10 DAYS THAT CHANGED AMERICA

VOLUME 2: BUILDING A NATION

About the Authors

Terry D. Bilhartz is a professor of history at Sam Houston State University who has taught about 18,000 students during his career. He is the author of more than 50 articles and book chapters in the fields of history, religion, philosophy, psychology, and medicine, and has written scripts for public television documentaries. He is the author of *Urban Religion and the Second Great Awakening*, *Francis Asbury's America*, *Images of Texas in the Nation* (with Paul Ruffin), *Constructing the American Past* (with Elliot Gorn and Randy Roberts), *Sacred Words: A Source Book on the Great Religions of the World*, and *Currents in American History* (with Alan Elliott). Bilhartz holds degrees from Dallas Baptist College (BS), Emory University (MA), and the George Washington University (PhD), and has completed post-doctoral studies in history and religion at Vanderbilt University, Stanford University, the University of Connecticut, the East-West Center at the University of Hawaii, and the Australian National University.

Alan C. Elliott is the Director of Statistical Consulting in the Department of Statistical Science at Southern Methodist University. He is the author of numerous academic articles and over 30 books on topics including science, history, and biography. Current books include *A Daily Dose of the American Dream*; *Texas Ingenuity: Inventions, Inventors & Innovators*; *Legendary Locals of Oak Cliff*; *Images of America: Oak Cliff*; and *Currents in American History* (with Terry Bilhartz.) Technical books include *SAS Essentials*, *Statistical Analysis Quick Reference Guidebook*, and *Applied Time Series Analysis*. He specializes in writing techniques designed to make challenging subjects easy to understand.

10 DAYS THAT CHANGED AMERICA

Volume 2: Building a Nation

Terry D. Bilhartz and Alan C. Elliott

2014
GREEN PUBLISHING HOUSE, LLC
College Station, Texas

10 Days That Changed America, Volume 2: Building a Nation

Copyright © 2014 by Green Publishing House, LLC

All rights reserved. Printed in the United States of America. No part of this book may be reproduced or distributed in any form or by any means, or stored in a database or retrieval system, without written permission from the publisher, Green Publishing House, LLD, including, but limited to, in any network or other electronic storage or transmission, or broadcast for distance learning.

Some ancillaries, including electronic and print components, may not be available to customers outside of the United States.

ISBN 978-1-63432-005-4 (paperback)
ISBN 978-1-63432-006-1 (ePub)
ISBN 978-1-63432-007-8 (pdf)
ISBN 978-1-63432-008-5 (mobi)
ISBN 978-1-63432-009-2 (audio)

The Internet addresses listed in the text were accurate at the time of publication. The inclusion of a website does not indicate an endorsement by the authors or Green Publishing House, LLC, and Green Publishing House does not guarantee the accuracy of the information presented at these sites.

www.GreenPublishingHouse.com

To our parents and mentors who considered us their children

Skipper and Joy Bilhartz
Tom Samford and Ida Scirratt Elliott
Joseph and Carol Abston
Paul and Ann Morell

About Green Publishing House, LLC

Green Publishing House is a Limited Liability Corporation dedicated to the production and global distribution of scholarly, peer-reviewed, academic books and high quality general interest trade books. Green Publishing House partners with numerous distributors to deliver valued books across multiple platforms (digital and print) at competitive costs.

The central mission of Green Publishing House is to deliver high quality digital textbooks and trade books to readers at low prices. Going digital is not only environmentally responsible and less expensive to readers, but it also offers our clients the opportunity to receive up-to-date scholarly resources on a moment's notice from millions of locations worldwide.

Although the number of digital readers is growing every year, because everyone may not have access to the internet and eBook readers, and because some individuals, book reviewers, and libraries may prefer hard copy texts, the company also offers print copies of its books. To remain loyal to its central mission, however, the company encourages the purchase of digital versions of its books, and cheerfully donates a portion of the revenue it receives from its print copy sales to educational and charitable institutions.

Detailed Table of Contents

Preface	1

Chapter 1:
History and Historians:
Making Sense of the Full Catastrophe of Life

A Concise Guide for Training Historians	7
What is History?	9
Envisioning a Time Before History	14
The Genesis of History	17
The Methods of History	21
Understanding Historical Questions & the Limits of History	24
It's About Time: The Agony & Ecstasy of Dating	29
It's About Integrity: The Ethics of Creating History	33
The Purpose and Structure of *10 Days*	35
Historians at Work: How to Use this Text	41
Probing the Sources: From Story to History	41
Document 1: Excerpts from Genesis (*KJV*)	42
Document 2: Excerpts from Herodotus, *The Histories*	43
What Others Say: Investigating Competing Historical Arguments	44
Document 1: Selected Quotes – Historians on History	46
Looking Backward/Looking Forward: Thinking Historically	49
Suggested Readings	50
Online Resources	51
A Premise and a Challenge	51

Chapter 5:
Defining the American Dream, July 2, 1776
The Declaration of Independence & the Forging of a New Nation

PRELUDE 55
   Conceived In Liberty – The Story Behind the Story 56
   The Long Road to Rebellion 67
THE BIG EVENT
   Decision Time, July 2, 1776 75
POSTLUDE
   Implementing the American Dream 82
   The Critical Period – The Economy of Impotence 86
   America Reinvents Itself 88
PROBING THE SOURCES: Three Revolutionary Visions:
   Common Sense, The Declaration of Independence,
   and the Constitution of 1787 93
   Document 1: Excerpts from Thomas Paine,
   Common Sense (1776) 93
   Document 2: Comparative Drafts of the Declaration
   of Independence 97
   Document 3: Excerpts from the Constitution of 1787
   (1787) 110
WHAT OTHERS SAY: Remembering the Declaration
   of Independence 125
   Document 1: Excerpts from the "Declaration of Rights
   and Sentiments" (1848) 126
   Document 2: Excerpts from Frederick Douglas, "What
   to a Slave is the Fourth of July?" (1852) 128
   Document 3: Abraham Lincoln, "The Gettysburg
   Address" (1863) 130
   Document 4: Excerpts from Pauline Maier, *American
   Scripture: Making the Declaration of Independence*
   (Alfred A Knopf, 1997) 131
   Document 5: Excerpts from David Armitage, *The
   Declaration of Independence: A Global History*
   (Harvard University Press, 2007) 133
LOOKING BACKWARD/LOOKING FORWARD:
   Who Supports What? 135
SUGGESTED READINGS 136

ONLINE RESOURCES 137

Chapter 6:
Undeclaring War, February 18, 1799:
Navigating Neutrality & the Ramifications
of the Pursuit of Peace

PRELUDE	141
Washington's Balancing Act – Liberty & Security	
In the Federalist Era	143
Foreign Affairs of the Federalist Era	150
By-Products of Jay's Treaty	153
Inherited Problems – Friction with France	158
THE BIG EVENT	
From Hawk to Dove – The Shifting Priorities of	
President John Adams	163
Decision Day and Its Immediate Aftermath	171
POSTLUDE	
Long Term Ramifications – The Ascendancy of	
Republicanism	176
Evaluating the Revolution of 1800	178
Other By-Products of Peace – The Louisiana	
Purchase	180
America In Search of Respect – The Limits	
of Neutrality	183
PROBING THE SOURCES: Questioning the Justice of	
Outlawing Opposition	187
Document 1: Excerpts from the Sedition Act of 1798	188
Document 2: Arguments Favoring the Sedition Act	191
Document 3: Arguments Opposing the Sedition Act	194
Document 4: Excerpts from the Kentucky Resolution	
of 1798	196
WHAT OTHERS SAY: The Revolution of 1800 and	
Its Limits	199
Document 1: Excerpts from Edward J. Larson,	
A Magnificent Catastrophe: The Tumultuous Election	
of 1800: America's First Presidential Campaign	
(Free Press, 2007)	200
Document 2: Excerpts from John Ferling, *Adams vs.*	

Jefferson: The Tumultuous Election of 1800
(Oxford University Press, 2004) 202
Document 3: Excerpts from Rosemarie Zagarri,
Revolutionary Backlash: Women and Politics in the Early American Republic (University of Pennsylvania Press, 2007) 204
LOOKING BACKWARD/LOOKING FORWARD:
Reflections on the Silent Majorities 206
SUGGESTED READINGS 208
ONLINE RESOURCES 208

Chapter 7:
Struggling for Survival, September 13, 1813: The Battle of Baltimore & the Emergence of American Nationalism

PRELUDE 211
   The 2nd American Revolution or
      Mr. Madison's War 215
   1812 – 1814: Years of Defeat and Disunion 219
THE BIG EVENT
   Turning the Tide – The Battle of Baltimore 223
   Negotiating the Treaty of Ghent – America's
      Christmas Gift 226
   The Battle of New Orleans – A Meaningless-
      Meaningful American Victory 233
POSTLUDE
   The Legacy of the War of 1812 236
   Politics in the Era of Good Feelings 238
   From Good Feelings to Bad – The Revival of
      Political Strife 242
PROBING THE SOURCES: Expressions of Unity and
      Disunity in the Early Republic 245
   Document 1: Constitutional Amendments Proposed
      By the Hartford Convention (1814/1815) 245
   Document 2: Excerpts from the Missouri
      Compromise (1820) 250
   Document 3: Excerpts from the Monroe Doctrine 259

WHAT OTHERS SAY: Making Sense of the
    War of 1812 — 265
  Document 1: Excerpts from Donald R. Hickey,
    The War of 1812: A Forgotten Conflict
    (University of Illinois Press, 1989) — 266
  Document 2: Excerpts from Alan Taylor, *The*
    Civil War of 1812: American Citizens, British
    Subjects, Irish Rebels, and Indian Allies
    (Alfred A. Knopf, 2010) — 268
  Document 3: Excerpts from Gene Alan Smith,
    The Slaves' Gamble: Choosing Sides in the
    War of 1812 (Palgrave Macmillan, 2013) — 270
LOOKING BACKWARD/LOOKING FORWARD:
  Constructing a National Narrative — 272
SUGGESTED READINGS — 273
ONLINE RESOURCES — 274

INDEX — 277

Preface

Sitting on my desk are three beautiful new editions of college history survey textbooks. I did not request these copies, but the publishers sent them to me to encourage me to adopt them in my classes. If I were to ask my one- and four-year-old grandsons, Carson and Peyton, to peruse these books and say a word that described them, I suspect the word that would come to their minds would be "heavy." If I were to ask my six-year-old grandson, Preston, the same question, he might add the descriptive word "colorful." These descriptions, "heavy" and "colorful," would be accurate because the average weight of these is about forty ounces, and multi-colors exist on almost every page. If I then were to ask college freshmen in a university book store to comment on these textbooks, I suspect their most common answer would be "expensive." This also would be an appropriate answer because the average 2014 price tags for these texts is about $130, an expensive investment for most college freshmen, even if this still is a lower price than textbooks in many other disciplines.

For me, an instructor who wants to instill my passion for history into the unfortunate students who don't want to take this course, but must do so in order to satisfy a degree requirement for their major, the words that I would use to describe these texts would be "comprehensive but scattered."

I say this because it seems to me that these works aspire to be magazine look-alike books that say something about every topic of interest to contemporary academic historians. In order to cover the whole waterfront of the American past in an aesthetically pleasing fashion, virtually every page of these texts supplements the historical narrative with etchings (i.e., modern drawings meant to look like historic artifacts), highlighted boxes containing timelines, isolated quotes, short biographies or an assortment of other interesting but disjointed historical tidbits, and maps, portraits, and illustrations that easily can be accessed and expanded to a more useful size with a simple internet search.

In some texts, these supplemental features fill about one-half of the space allotted to each chapter. Valuable content is contained in these supplemental features, but according to adult learning theory, this content would more likely be delivered and retained if students played a more active role in constructing this content for themselves rather than simply having it presented to them in disjointed segments.

I am not opposed to the creation of artfully designed, full-color, comprehensive, and expensive textbooks that also can duplicate as attractive coffee table books to adorn home libraries and living rooms. In fact, I have been the author of such textbooks with some of the same publishing houses.

However, after spending several decades in the classroom experimenting with ways to make the past come alive to students – many of whom arrive with little initial interest in history – and for part of that time serving simultaneously as a college administrator concerned with the rising price of textbooks, I no longer embrace a "more is better" educational philosophy.

My years of experience teach me that streamlined, pedagogically focused, and environmentally and consumer friendly textbooks offer more economic and educational value to students than beautiful, heavy, and expensive comprehensive textbooks.

10 Days That Changed America intertwines with its narrative primary sources, historiographical essays, and problem-based learning exercises. Yet these features are not mere add-ons, but are essential to the design of each chapter. The purpose of this textbook is not only to present a narrative of the past in a lively and readable style that can be digested and remembered by its readers, but it also is to train students how to do the work of historians. Every page of the volume is designed with this end.

Although Green Publishing House also offers hard copy versions of this textbook, *10 Days That Changed*

America was written to be read on an eBook reader. Therefore, it uses shorter paragraphs and makes greater use of abbreviations in headings than is standard protocol for hardcover books. Pieces of this text were originally published in a more standard textbook format as *Currents in American History* (ME Sharpe, 2007).

The authors of this text would like to extend their thanks to a network of friends and colleagues who have helped to make this work possible. Special thanks goes to professors Rosanne Barker, Ty Cashion, Caroline Crimm, Yvonne Frear, Katherine Gaskamp, Jeff Littlejohn, James Olson, Darren Pierson, Bernadette Pruitt, Blake Tritico, and Susannah Ural for not only reviewing early drafts, but also on occasions piloting portions of the text with some of their students. We also thank Rocky Bilhartz, Lindsey Bilhartz, Patty Bilhartz, Bob and Carol Bogart, Steve Drummond, Mary Elliott, William Elliott, Betty Gore, Kyle Longley, Scott Maxwell, Teri Maxwell, Bryant Simon, LenPaul Stadler, Michael L. Tate, and Wayne Woodward who assisted us as proofreaders and friendly critics. We also thank the academic historians initially known to us only by their insightful comments who reviewed early drafts of this work.

Finally, to the students who will be asked by their teachers to read this text, the authors of this textbook would like to send you a challenge. At the end of the semester, no matter what opinions you hold, we encourage you to send to the Green Publishing House website your thoughts about history in general and about this textbook in particular. Did reading this text change your attitude about history? Did it help you to become a better historian? Specifically, what pieces of the text did you find to be most and least helpful? What changes would you recommend in future editions?

The insights you provide will be helpful to both future students and to the authors of this text. And for those who offer constructive criticism, do not be surprised if the next edition of this textbook incorporates some of your ideas.

From the desk of

Terry D. Bilhartz
Professor of History
Sam Houston State University
July 2014

Chapter 1:

History and Historians:

Making Sense of the Full Catastrophe of Life

A Concise Guide for Training Historians

Hundreds of graduating seniors surrounded by two thousand supporting guests crammed into a university coliseum for a spring graduation. The speaker on this occasion was a distinguished physician who grew up in San Antonio, Texas, the son of hardworking Mexican immigrants. As a young man he was a gifted athlete, earning All-American honors as a receiver on his college's football team. After a brief stint in the NFL, he pursued a career in medicine, gaining international recognition as an expert in the field of sports-related facial injuries.

He opened his address by telling the graduates that each of them would leave the building with something that no one else would have. This gift was not a diploma, for thousands of others on that day would receive this honor. Instead, the unique gift that was given to each graduate was the privilege of being in charge of his or her own destiny. The speaker followed with standard platitudes fitted to this occasion, telling the graduates to shoot for the stars, to work hard to reach their dreams, to learn from mentors who would assist them along the way, and to remember as their guide Booker T. Washington's definition of achievement: "Success is to be measured not so much by the position that one has reached in life as by the obstacles which one has overcome."

While the speaker's words were well-articulated, what made the address so powerful was the way he illustrated each point with stories from his own life. To illustrate his final point, for example, he spoke about an incident that occurred during his medical residency when he traveled to a remote region of Brazil to perform facial reconstruction surgeries on the indigenous population. Unfortunately, on this occasion an infant child who underwent a cleft lip repair perished on his operating table. Frustrated at the loss of his first patient, the surgeon tore off his surgical gloves and started to leave the makeshift jungle clinic when his mentor ordered him to return to the table, finish the surgical repair, and carry the deceased child back to his parents.

With a somber tone, the speaker recounted his memory of the parents' reaction to the tragic news. Although deeply saddened, the parents found some comfort in gazing at the face of their baby because, as was the custom in their village, they believed that while God would never accept a blemished child into paradise, they felt that their now beautiful baby had been transported to heaven.

Only moments after the speaker finished his remarks, someone in the coliseum audience slumped in his seat. Seeing the distress of the subject from the podium, the physician speaker swiftly left the stage to attend to the medical needs of the stricken man. As people in the crowd strained their necks to get a glimpse of what was happening, a hush filled the coliseum, until someone looking down from the upper tier broke the silence by shouting out to one of the graduates below. This outburst triggered another shout from the bleachers. Although the Master-of-Ceremonies on the podium asked the crowd to be patient while the stricken man was receiving care, this request for decorum had little effect, as growing numbers in the audience used the pause in the ceremonies to dance and wave and shout words of celebration to the cap-and-gown-dressed graduates below. The catcalls quieted only when uniformed officers placed themselves more visibly in the aisles of the coliseum. Meanwhile, one faculty member experiencing the moment remarked to himself: "The human race, is all over the place."

WHAT IS HISTORY?

If a historian were asked to research and produce an interpretive account of this commencement exercise, what type of research would the historian conduct, and what would the outline of the finished history product look like? Perhaps the most accurate answer to this question would be the simple response: there are multiple valid answers to this question.

To illustrate, most historians tasked with this assignment would be quick to gather additional evidence by locating any extant recordings of the event, by securing the commencement program with its lists of graduating students, and by conducting oral interviews with the graduating students and their friends and family who attended the event. The type of information scholars would glean from these new sources, however, as well as the types of secondary sources they would consult to provide context and significance to the event, would likely vary according to the interests, perspectives, and historical training of each historian.

A biographer, for instance, might be fascinated with the life details of the commencement speaker, and how his recipe for success and life experiences seemed to echo what others have referred to as "the American dream." A social historian might be more critical of the utility of the commencement speaker's advice, and contrast his biography with the lives of thousands of other children of Mexican immigrants whose lives did not follow the same trajectory as the speaker because of unmentioned and dissimilar social determinants. Another historian also might question the universality of the speaker's advice by noting that the ability to set goals and develop work and networking patterns to accomplish them is largely determined by chemical reactions at the cellular level, processes that are determined less by self-will than by inheritance, nutrition, and chance.

Still other historians might frame their histories around other details. A cultural historian with anthropological interests, for example, might choose to explore the rituals that were being practiced and violated during the commencement exercise, while a quantitative historian with sociological leanings might prefer to survey groups of people for their attitudes regarding the commencement speech and the commotion on the floor in an attempt to understand if these attitudes were influenced by age, gender, ethnicity, and economic class. Still others might seek to explore what the faculty observer meant when he reflected, "The human race, is all over the place."

In sum, if an account of a contemporaneous one-hour event taking place within a single building can produce such diverse histories, should we not expect to find that narratives of life in the past also will be complex stories of affairs that can be expressed in many different forms? This is not to suggest that there is no rubric that can be used to separate what constitutes compelling historical arguments from unpersuasive ones, but this does suggest that historians, perhaps more so than scholars trained in harder sciences, are generally comfortable acknowledging that there may be a variety of historically contingent routes to any particular event, and that meaningful insights can be gained from multiple investigative methodologies. Events of the past and records of these events may be concrete and unchanging, like the actual commencement ceremony and a video tape of it, but how historians record and explain these events is anything but uniform and static.

This work is based on these premises:

> *Historians exist, not to memorize and regurgitate the past, but to create "history."*

> *The primary objective of history survey courses is NOT to teach students everything they need to know about history, but to help them become historians.*

> *Historians of America understand that stories of the American past include complex and fascinating tales of intrigue, adventure, irony, and fulfilled and unfulfilled dreams that offer insight into why Americans think and behave as they do.*

If you do not fully agree with these assertions, you should realize that you are in good company because few students taking an introductory course in American history start the semester with this understanding. Actually, if you are skeptical of the truth of these statements, you have a disposition that would suit you well as a history student because historians are trained to become deliberative, creative thinkers not easily persuaded by authoritative claims, especially those presented without evidential support.

Thinking historically requires one to have the curiosity of a detective, and to maintain an open mind that seeks not so much to find agreement with but to understand foreign ideas, even if those ideas at face value sound absurd. As non-gullible, truth-seeking investigators, historians must strive to develop the skills that will enable them to view objects and ideas from multiple perspectives, and to understand how even arguments and behaviors that seem unintelligible to most conventional minds could be embraced by other peoples.

The authors of this book agree that the assertion that historians "create history" appears nonsensical for some critical thinkers who rightly insist that humans living at this moment do not possess the superpowers necessary to create the past. This point we concede, but our claim is not that historians create the actual past that was once experienced, but that historians create "history." In the following paragraphs we will attempt to clarify what we mean when we use the word "history." Understanding the distinction between what we call "history" and the actual past is central to understanding our central proposition that historians create history.

ENVISIONING A TIME BEFORE HISTORY

At various points in this text we will invite you to put down your eBook or book, or to hit the pause button on your audio-book reader device, in order to stop and reflect on a statement or a set of questions. Whenever you see the words "PAUSE-REFLECT-THINK" we encourage you to deliberate a moment on the idea before you.

In the next few moments, go on a mental journey by giving some thought to the following:

Envision a time before history. As you contemplate this idea, what images come to your mind? Moving forward, what prerequisites must exist for history to arise?

PAUSE-REFLECT-THINK

Most of us, when first asked to reflect on a time before history, create in our minds images of darkness, dinosaurs, or hairy Neanderthals. These images are accurate, but when thinking these thoughts, we probably are assuming that history means "the past" or, more specifically, "the human past." Although "the past" is indeed a definition of history, it is not the only definition. When students major in history, for instance, they do not major in "the past." Instead, they major in a subject or in a branch of knowledge known as "history."

Thus, "history," in this more technical sense, is not the past, but rather is a perception of the past that has been constructed by following a process that is often referred to as "the historical method." This method involves applying rules of evidence to sources (such as artifacts, letters on a page, audio recordings, physical visual images, etc.) that date to some distant time and place being studied. Historians (students of the past who practice this craft) call these distant sources "primary sources." The craft or method of history in its most basic form is an attempt to understand what life was like in the past by applying reasoned arguments to primary source materials.

History is not the only way to make sense of the past. Long before there were historians there were mythmakers who told stories of past times that explained how things came to be as they are. Recognizing this leads us to another set of questions:

When did people start trusting the historical method as the most reliable way to make sense of the past? In short, how old is history? Who invented it and why? And how has this approach to the past influenced the way modern Americans think and act?

These simple questions have complex answers that may surprise even serious students of history. Not yet even 2,500 years old, history as a discipline is not as old as many think. Neither is it universally recognized as the most credible way to explain life in the past. Indeed, even in the 21st century indigenous populations can be found on every continent that have no desire to use reasoned arguments drawn from primary sources to make sense of their past.

Yet, although a relatively new human invention, and one that still has not convinced all peoples of its value, the craft of history has had a profound impact on how peoples familiar with Western civilization, and more recently with Eastern civilization as well, think critically. In fact, the influence of history on how we organize our place in time is so engrained in our culture that many educated Americans find it difficult to approach the past in any other way.

To begin the search for the origins of history, at least for North Americans familiar with the advance of Western civilization, there is no better place to start than to investigate the ancient book that opens with the familiar line: "In the beginning God created the heavens and the earth."

THE GENESIS OF HISTORY

In this story from the book of Genesis, a work sacred to many that is contained in both the Hebrew and Christian Bibles, God speaks, creates, declares the creation to be good, and then calls it evening and morning, the end of day one. As the story continues, God speaks again, creating more than previously existed, declares the new creation to be good, and then calls it evening and morning, the end of day two. After more creations on days three, four, five, and six, God rests and declares the seventh day to be holy.

The Genesis story continues with a well-known account involving the characters Adam and Eve. This story and the subsequent Hebrew sacred stories make the point that human actions have consequences that can spoil the goodness of creation, but that obedience to the creator of life can bring blessings. To the ancient Hebrews, human decisions and actions were important and carried even sacred, ontological significance.

Although many other ancient peoples also had creation stories, the Genesis account has had the more profound influence on the development of Western Civilization. Genesis is important not because scholars consider it superior history or science (indeed, it was composed long before either of these disciplines was invented), but because it takes a novel approach to time and because it gives importance to the consequences of human activity.

Unlike the ancient Hebrews, other ancient peoples often passed down sacred stories that operated outside what moderns would call historic time and place. Many of the great stories of Greek mythology, for example, take place in the skies of Mount Olympus or at the bottom of the sea. In contrast, most of the activities in the Hebrew Bible take place at ground level, in a world that seems mostly recognizable to modern eyes.

More importantly, according to many ancients from both the East and the West, time did not flow forward as much as it moved in a circle like the spinning of a wheel. The sacred stories of many peoples from India to the Americas suggested that just as the sun followed its daily course and the moon followed its monthly rhythms, humans were born, matured, died, and then were returned back into a recycling cosmos. In cultures with sacred myths that viewed time as cyclic, there was less incentive to record daily activities or to fret about daily decisions. In an eternal cosmos with no beginning or end, but only transitions, the struggle to improve creation appeared to be an impossible and even unwanted ideal.

Unlike these contemporaries, however, the ancient Hebrews viewed time linearly and gave credence to the idea of progress. Time flowing forward from the past to the present in a straight line progression did not necessarily imply human progress, because regression also could occur, but it did at least suggest the possibility of improvement.

The sacred stories in the Hebrew Bible are principally theological compositions about the relationship between these people and their God. However, owing to the Hebrew construction of linear time and discussion of the cosmic events within earthly space, the ancient Hebrew narratives look more familiar to modern readers of history than many other ancient texts. The Hebrews did not invent the discipline we now call history, but their approach to time and place did lay the foundation for it.

History – that is, the intellectual discipline that uses reasoned evidence from extant sources to make sense of the past – owes its origins not to the Hebrews, but to the Greeks. The evolution of this discipline was slow. In the sixth century BCE, a few Greek thinkers became dissatisfied with the traditional mythological explanations for the creation of the cosmos from the activities of the gods. Trusting observation and reason over their sacred mysteries, these Greeks attempted to explain the natural world without making reference to the supernatural. With these investigations into the physical world, science, or at least a distant relative of it, was born.

About a century later, Herodotus, another Greek intellectual unconvinced by the explanations of the myths, determined to understand how society as he knew it came to be. Specifically, he wanted to understand the causes of the Greek-Persian War, the foremost event that framed the time in which he lived. Herodotus traveled to distant lands, looking for sources – some written, but mostly oral – that could help him find his answers. When his sources offered suggestions that defied observation and logic, he rejected them, demanding instead more reasonable explanations. Herodotus published his findings in a work entitled *The Histories,* a word that literally meant "inquiry" or "research." With this publication, Herodotus invented the genre of history.

Many readers today will not embrace the theology of the ancient Hebrews or the philosophies of the ancient Greeks, but most will accept the Hebraic arrangement of linear time and the Greek demand for causation arguments based on rational analysis of sources. This is because Western Civilization has been largely influenced by the ideas of the ancient Hebrews and Greeks. Like the precursors and creators of the discipline of history, most modern Americans view time as a continuous stream of forward moving, nonreversible events, with each event being both a product of previous actions and a force that influences the possibilities of future events. The present builds on the past, and every moment in time is shaped by it.

THE METHODS OF HISTORY

Since the time of Herodotus, critical thinkers whom we call historians have chosen to rely on the trustworthiness of linear time and on the necessity of using reason to unpack clues contained in primary sources as the most credible ways to understand the past and its relationship to the present. No universally accepted guidebook listing rules that historians must follow has been canonized. Historians, in short, do not embrace a single instruction book or bible that tells them how to make sense of the past.

Indeed, historians of different stripes and from different eras have disagreed and continue to disagree on a number of basic issues related to the purposes, scope, presentation and citation format, and methods of historical inquiry. Historians also have expressed and continue to express differing opinions regarding the objective versus the subjective nature of history, the constancy or cultural relativity of human nature, and whether history is better described as an art or a science. Exploring how and why historians disagree about both content and method is itself an intellectually stimulating field of study that historians have named "historiography." More will be said about this interesting field later in this volume.

Yet while historians disagree about many things, when asked to describe what they do and how they do it, most historians would share several common answers. One way to condense these common practices is to present them in a five step format that is compatible with the teaching style of instructors who embrace a project-based learning pedagogy.

These basic steps include:

(1) assimilate some knowledge about a segment of the past that has been suggested by critical thinkers who have carefully investigated the subject;

(2) create a probing question, the answers to which will build on or revise that conventionally accepted knowledge;

(3) compose a "need to know" list of background materials and sources from the era being studied that contains clues about the past relevant to the question at hand;

(4) extract and analyze information contained in these sources, expelling the irrelevant and less trustworthy information, and arranging the more pertinent information in some meaningful way that communicates a vision of the past; and

HISTORY AND HISTORIANS 23

(5) construct a "history" by artfully publishing (which means "to circulate widely") an account of the past that can be comprehended by a targeted audience.

By reading this book with the eyes of a broad- and open-minded truth seeker; by releasing your imagination to create probing questions about the American past that excite your curiosity; by scavenging for primary sources that may offer clues to help you find answers to these questions; by extracting, analyzing, selecting, and organizing pertinent information obtained from these sources; and by artfully presenting your vision of the past to others, you not only will develop the skills of a historian, but you also will create history.

Be forewarned. No matter how long you practice this craft, you will never learn everything that is worth knowing about the past. The best that you can hope for is to become an expert in segments of the past, not the past in its entirety. The good news, however, is that most who begin a mental journey into the past will find the experience to be more rewarding than originally imagined. In fact, this book should come with a warning label: "creating history" can become addictive and change your life!

Before you start on this intellectual journey into the American past, it would be wise to be aware of some of the common pitfalls that often cause beginner historians to stumble. Here are some helpful hints to assist you on your journey into the past.

UNDERSTANDING HISTORICAL QUESTIONS & THE LIMITS OF HISTORY

To begin, you need to understand the scope and acknowledge the limitations of the historical method. While history is a powerful tool that can offer us insight into many things, it is not the only worthy branch of knowledge, and it cannot address all questions that are worthy of human interest.

Positioned on opposing sides of the discipline of history are two other ways to communicate truth: science and myth. Science, a discipline that gathers knowledge about the physical universe through observation and experimentation, aspires to discover general laws that can explain current natural phenomena and also, when the precise conditions are reproduced, to predict with accuracy future phenomena. The method of science is rigorous and its scope is limited to explorations of the material cosmos, not to the supernatural.

Myth also seeks to explain the origins of natural phenomena or aspects of human behavior, but unlike science, it is unfettered by method, and the scope of myth is limitless as there are no questions that it cannot seek to answer. The purpose of myth is to communicate the truth believed by a culture through the retelling of a traditional story.

In many ways history is located somewhere on a spectrum between science and myth. History is a branch of knowledge that is more concerned with unique, particular events than is science, and it therefore does not generally pronounce general laws that can predict future events. Like scientific truth, however, historical truth will not be accepted if its arguments are deemed to include "unreasonable" explanations.

Moreover, because the discipline of history is dependent on evidence contained in sources, historians cannot offer responses to questions for which there is no evidence. Although historians should aspire to find evidence to reconstruct all segments of the past, some past experiences may never be recovered. The past exists without sources, but without sources, there can be no history, at least by our definition of the word.

Sometimes uncertainties about the authenticity and/or the credibility of the sources rather than the lack of sources cloud our vision of the past. Because primary sources are historians' links to the past, when these links are broken by source authenticity or credibility questions, the historians' arguments, no matter how artfully presented, will not be compelling.

Determining the authenticity of the source – that is, who produced the source and when – is necessary to ensure that the source truly is what it purports to be and not a forgery or garbled reproduction that shares little in common with the original. Professional historians, especially those studying eras before the invention of the printing press, have always been cognizant of the need to check on the authenticity of sources, but in the modern age of the internet, anyone who uses digital search engines to conduct research must never forget this step in the historical process. Do not be gullible. Before you accept a source, especially a source found on an internet site, first do your homework, and do not use it until you are confident that it is an authentic primary source.

After determining that a source is authentic, the next step is to assess its credibility. Just because an eyewitness leaves an account of an event (thereby creating a primary source), this does not mean that this eyewitness offers a trustworthy testimony. After all, the source could have been intentionally produced to mislead future investigators. More likely, the source could have been an honest attempt at assessment that captured only a part of the truth or simply missed the mark entirely.

Determining how much credibility you give to each source is a judicious process. To help you reach your verdict about the credibility of a source, you may want to ask yourself some of the following questions:

> For whom did the author produce the source? Did the author intend it to be published and read by future investigators? How close – both in proximity and in relationship – was the author to the subject being described? Did the author have the skills and knowledge to provide expert testimony? Did the author rely on memory or on other sources while creating the account? How much time passed between the event and the author's testimony about it?

While assessing the credibility of a source can be a subjective process, by reflecting on questions such as these you will become a better detective and thereby become a better historian.

Beginner historians should not be surprised to find that even authentic and credible sources may not always converge with each other. One of the fundamental skills that historians must master is the ability to weigh, arrange, and integrate conflicting testimony. Fortunately, to a greater degree than newspaper journalists and CNN analysts who often must report breaking news as it unfolds, historians have the freedom and the responsibility to deliberatively reflect on multiple sources from multiple perspectives before rendering their judgments.

Another basic concept that historians must know is that the historical method cannot offer answers to all questions that might excite their curiosity. Consequently, when you create probing questions to study, you should avoid questions for which primary source evidence cannot be found, including, for instance, timeless existential questions like "what is the meaning of life?" or "what if" questions such as "would slavery have been abolished within fifty years if the Confederacy had won the Civil War?"

If your imagination draws you to these types of questions, do not abandon those thoughts and interests, but find ways to reframe non-historical questions into historical ones. For example, rather than asking the timeless question "what is the nature of God?", turn the question into a historical one located in time and place by asking "according to the Hebrew peoples at the time of Ezra, what was the nature of God?"

IT'S ABOUT TIME: THE AGONY & ECSTASY OF DATING

Another basic idea beginner historians need to understand is that history is a branch of knowledge that is fundamentally about time or, more precisely, timing. In comparison with science, history is a flexible discipline, welcoming multiple answers to the questions that it poses. There is one methodological rule, however, that is inviolable. What is this great commandment, this unalterable law? *Historians must agree that historic time is irreversible and, therefore, more recent events cannot be said to influence more distant ones.* To reverse the timing of events is to misconstrue the past.

Because placing things appropriately in time is so crucial to historical understanding, historians must become "dating" experts and therefore need to be aware of potential dating problems. Like real life dating, learning to date historically can be more complicated than it first appears, and can lead to horrific experiences if not done well. Thus, to help beginner historians create "history," here are a couple of recommended dating techniques that you may want to incorporate into your practice.

Dating tip one: realize that simply placing events on a timeline without referencing them to each other should be avoided unless your purpose in creating history is to treat insomnia.

The reason that making dates the focal point of your history is so deadly is because it is listless and boring, it offers little historical insight into the period being studied, and it actually can be misleading to your readers. Most readers of this work probably do not need to be convinced by our first two points, but regarding the third point, consider this. Placing events into a historical calendar can be confusing because there actually is no universally agreed on way to locate events in time.

The calendar that most of us use every day is the Gregorian, or Western Calendar. This calendar declares a year to consist of 365 days (except in leap-years when the number is 366) that are assigned to twelve months of 28 to 31 days in length, with the years being numbered in units before and after the estimated time of the birth of Jesus of Nazareth. Although this dating system is widely known around the world, it is not the only dating timeline currently in use.

To make the dating of events even more complicated, this current Gregorian calendar, which was recommended in 1582 by Pope Gregory XIII, revised an earlier Julian Calendar by refining how often leap years would be added to the calendar, and by moving the days of the calendar year forward so that the season of the year would be aligned with the seasons that existed in the year 325 when Emperor Constantine called Christian bishops to gather at Nicaea for the First Ecumenical Council. While Roman Catholic regions immediately adopted Pope Gregory's recommendations, generations would pass before non-Catholic regions accepted the Gregorian reforms. In fact, the last European nation embraced the new dating system only in 1923. Consequently, between 1582 and 1923, different dating systems were concurrently being used in different world regions, thereby creating potential confusion for those attempting to place events in time.

Here is one example of how duplicate dating systems can result in confusion. If a historian of literary giants stated that both Shakespeare and Cervantes died on April 23, 1616, she/he would be correct, although this statement, if offered without context, would be misleading because Shakespeare, in fact, lived ten days longer than Cervantes. They share a common date of death only because Shakespeare lived in England, which at the time followed the Old Style Julian Calendar, while Cervantes lived in Spain, which at that time had already embraced the New Style Gregorian Calendar.

This example reminds us that we need to carefully interpret distant sources, remembering that when arranging events in order, we must take into account whether the reference is using the Old Style (Julian) calendar, the New

Style (Gregorian) calendar, or some other dating system. Because this volume focuses mostly on British North America after 1752, the year England shifted from the Julian to the Gregorian calendar, in this second volume of the series we standardize all dates to the New Style Gregorian Calendar. In our first volume, our dating was set to the Old Style Julian Calendar.

Dating tip two: don't obsess about giving a label to the time that something happened, but explore what it was that made that moment special.

Time flows steadily, and history is about time, but this does not mean that historians must treat all moments of time equally. To illustrate this point, think about a moment that was especially meaningful to you, such as a day you hit a homerun, played in a recital, won an award, graduated from school, or suffered the loss of a loved one or pet. Now think about what you were doing three days before that event. Most likely, coming up with an answer to the second question is more difficult than remembering an answer to the first, even though each of these days contained the same number of seconds. If one were to construct a history of your life from your perspective, most likely it would be appropriate to give more space to the moments that were meaningful to you, not to some arbitrary times before those events.

To capture life in its fullest, historians need to be able first to identify and arrange meaningful events in their proper sequence, and then to connect the dots, developing thematic and geographical as well as chronological associations between these events. Through backward linking, historians search for the origins or causes of meaningful moments. Through forward linking, historians investigate the significance or consequences of critical times. In telling the story of a critical moment or in writing a comparative history, historians also establish contemporaneous linkages by creating parallel time charts and observing similarities and differences between whatever aspects of life pertinent to the topic are being investigated. The more dots that can be connected, and the more interconnected associations that can be drawn, the more visual, colorful, and precise the vision of the past will be. Piecing segments of the past together to make a meaningful whole is a complex task, but it need not be a dreadful experience. Indeed, having a romance with "historical dating" can have its pleasures and rewards.

IT'S ABOUT INTEGRITY: THE ETHICS OF CREATING HISTORY

History will continue to be recognized as a credible discipline only as long as historians are respected as people with integrity. As curious truth seekers, historians must never forget that their central task is to convey a truthful understanding of the past that is not intentionally misleading. Although individual biases may be difficult to remove completely, the proper method of historical inquiry is not to reach a conclusion about the past and then search for and carefully select evidence that will support that conclusion. This may be the central motive of political spin advisors for candidates running for office, but it is contrary to the motivations of Clio, the mythical muse of history. Remember, probing questions should come first, followed by answers based on the ensuing research; not the reverse.

To retain integrity and maintain credibility, historians also must avoid constructing a history more elaborate than the evidence warrants. While ethical scholars in any discipline would never contemplate fabricating data out of thin air, in the rush to publish an idea first, or to present an argument in a more developed stage than the evidence allows, some may be tempted to overstate their arguments. Historians with integrity should avoid this temptation. It is appropriate, and indeed a necessity, to present a thesis that forcefully and artfully articulates a vision of the past, but authoritative assertions should not exceed the evidence that supports them.

Plagiarism, another unethical conduct that historians must avoid, is often committed more by laziness and sloppiness than by intention. But whether committed intentionally or by ignorance, appropriating the ideas of others as one's own and borrowing expressions without appropriate acknowledgment of their original sources are serious ethical offenses that can tarnish a career and lead to personal embarrassment and even legal penalties. Avoid this hazard at all costs.

THE PURPOSE AND STRUCTURE OF *10 DAYS THAT CHANGED AMERICA*

Just as the United States of America is an unfinished nation, *10 Days That Changed America* is presented as an unfinished work. The text offers a model that demonstrates on nine occasions how human decisions and activities on a given day transformed America in profound and sometimes tragic ways. To complete the work promised in the title, however, a future historian will need to locate another epoch-making moment in America's past, and create a compelling history that explains how the events of that momentous day evolved and were resolved, and how this resolution itself produced ripples that affected the lives of ensuing generations of Americans.

Every page of this text is designed to motivate and train a future historian to complete this task.

To help transform students into historians, each chapter of *10 Days That Changed America* contains the following parts:

(1) A "DAY THAT CHANGED AMERICA" narrative of a trigger-point moment that shaped the course of America.

Each narrative (a) sets the stage for a decisive event in a prelude section by discussing causes and pertinent preliminary influences that preceded the event, (b) describes the activities that took place during this great event by telling a dramatic story of that turning point moment, and (c) assesses the consequence and significance of the event in a postlude section by outlining the immediate and long-term impact of that crucial moment on ensuing generations.

The pivotal turning point events included in this text help students to learn how historians can frame a story of the past by selecting critical moments in American history and then through backward and forward linking analyses, describe the causes and consequences of these times.

The nine turning point days presented in the text illustrate *one* way of framing the contours of the American past from its colonial beginnings through the era of the Civil War and Reconstruction. Some of the nine "The Big Event" days, like the day that Europeans made first contact with the indigenous people who lived on the island Columbus named "San Salvador," are symbolic days that altered life only minimally at that precise moment but over time produced momentous consequences. Other selections, like the day the colonists declared their independence from Britain, brought immediate far-reaching consequences. Some days, like the day the Confederates bombarded Fort Sumter, thus triggering the Civil War, are events well-known by most American school children, while other days, like the date that President John Adams decided to pursue peace with France, may be little known even by professional historians.

The purpose of selecting this particular collection of days is not to suggest that these are the only or even the most important trigger moments in American history. Indeed, throughout the semester students will be encouraged to critique the selections of these days, and to reflect on and present other ways to arrange events and retell a meaningful story of the American past.

Nor is the purpose of this text to suggest that historians must frame the past around events, indeed, single-day events, although it does demonstrate that it is possible to structure a history of the American past around a brief number of twenty-four hour time periods.

Rather, the turning point events included in this work are selected purely for pedagogical reasons. By studying the causes of these events, and by understanding how the consequences of these events altered the world landscape in ways that prepared America for other future turning point moments, students will learn how to piece together the segments of the American past into a meaningful whole, and by doing so, will learn how to become historians.

(2) A "Probing the Sources" section that provides a collection of primary source documents pertinent to the central narrative discussed in the chapter.

Because primary sources are the building blocks of history, each chapter presents readers with an opportunity to analyze for themselves pertinent sources related to the central chapter topic. Introductory remarks provide readers with the context needed to approach the documents. Questions guide students through an exploration of the texts as they learn how to extract clues from, critique the reliability of, and organize trustworthy information about life in the past from primary source materials.

(3) A "What Others Say" section that introduces students to the historiography of pertinent secondary sources related to the central narrative discussed in the chapter.

By examining excerpts or summary arguments from the works of historians who have studied the central topic of the chapter, students will be challenged to (a) evaluate and critique secondary source materials, and (b) understand how secondary sources provide readers not only with a perspective of the topic being studied, but also with insight on the life and times of the historians themselves.

(4) A "Looking Backward/Looking Forward" section that challenges students to embark on an individual and/or group project learning assignment that builds on content presented in the chapter.

At the conclusion of each chapter, students will be encouraged to develop their historical skills by exploring in more detail one segment of the past that was only briefly introduced in the chapter narrative. Each chapter will focus on at least one skill set that historians need to master. Recommended topics and suggested probing questions will guide students through this journey into the past. One individual exercise and one project-based learning assignment will be suggested in each chapter.

(5) A "PAUSE-REFLECT-THINK" feature interspersed throughout the text encourages critical thinking and active reading by leading students toward self-reflection and inquiry before inundating them with too many facts.

To promote healthy vision, optometrist Dr. Stephen Means recommends that avid readers and those glued to computer screens all day follow this simple 20/20/20 rule: every 20 minutes, gaze for 20 seconds at a distance of at least 20 feet away. The "PAUSE-REFLECT-THINK" feature inserted throughout this volume encourages this healthy habit even as it challenges students to develop another useful habit – the habit of adding self-reflection or "think time" to their learning experiences.

According to adult learning theory, students remain unmotivated and resist learning when they feel others are imposing information on them, but they become engaged learners when given the opportunity to apply their existing knowledge to new learning experiences. By asking students to periodically stop their reading in order to reflect on and react to a historical argument or unconventional idea, this feature promotes active participation even during the reading of the text.

(6) A "Suggested Readings" section that provides bibliographies of recommended sources available in print and digital versions.

(7) An "Online Resources" section that recommends websites that contain maps, illustrations, tables, and other types of information that is pertinent to the chapter. Although all of the sites listed in this section were live and approved by authors at

the time of the release of this work, because we do not control these sites, we cannot guarantee the quality of the content on these sites.

HISTORIANS AT WORK: HOW TO USE THIS TEXT

The following paragraphs illustrate how each section of the text is designed to build on and stimulate greater student interaction with the conceptual material presented in the chapter.

PROBING THE SOURCES: Moving from Story to History

In our earlier discussions about the origins of history, we made brief references to two sources, the Book of Genesis that is contained in the Hebrew and Christian Bibles and *The Histories* that was written by Herodotus and published around 440 BCE. To dig deeper into these texts, in this section we offer some introductory comments about these sources and provide short excerpts from each of them.

Scholars generally characterize the Genesis account as a traditional story that serves to express the worldview of a people. The technical term for such an account is "myth," but do not confuse this use of the word "myth" with the popular notion of an unfounded or false notion. Myth, in this technical sense, is a story with a point. It is a way to communicate a truth through story-telling.

Many consider Herodotus's *The Histories*, written by the so-called "father of history," as the work that created the genre we call history. As you compare these works, consider how the purposes and the methods of the authors of these pieces are similar and different. Based on your reading of these sources, what constitutes some differences between sacred stories (or myths) and history?

Document 1: Excerpts from Genesis 12:1-5 The Calling of Abram (Abraham)

> Now the LORD had said unto Abram, Get thee out of thy country, and from thy kindred, and from thy father's house, unto a land that I will shew thee: And I will make of thee a great nation, and I will bless thee, and make thy name great; and thou shalt be a blessing: And I will bless them that bless thee, and curse him that curseth thee: and in thee shall all families of the earth be blessed.
> So Abram departed, as the LORD had spoken unto him; and Lot went with him: and Abram was seventy and five years old when he

departed out of Haran. And Abram took Sarai his wife, and Lot his brother's son, and all their substance that they had gathered, and the souls that they had gotten in Haran; and they went forth to go into the land of Canaan; and into the land of Canaan they came.

[This translation was taken from the King James Version of the Christian Bible that was first published in 1611. If you would like to continue reading in Genesis or other books in the Hebrew and Christian Bibles, you can access these materials free of charge on many websites. A convenient site that allows you to select the translation of your choice can be found at: http://www.biblegateway.com]

Document 2: Excerpts from Herodotus, *The Histories*: Herodotus's Approach to the Past

Herodotus of Halicarnassus, his *Researches* are here set down to preserve the memory of the past by putting on record the astonishing achievements both of our own and of other peoples; and more particularly, to show how they came into conflict.

Learned Persians put the responsibility for the quarrel on the Phoenicians.... Such then is the Persian story. In their view it was the capture of Troy that first made them enemies of the Greeks.... [T]he Phoenicians do not accept the Persians' account; they deny that they took her to Egypt by force....

So much for what Persians and Phoenicians say; and I have no intention of passing judgment on its truth or falsity. I prefer to rely on my own knowledge, and to point out who it was in actual fact that first injured the Greeks...

[This excerpt is from Aubrey de Selincourt's translation of *The Histories*. For an inexpensive full text of this translation, see the 1972 Penguin Classics revised edition that comes with an introduction and notes by A. R. Burn.]

WHAT OTHERS SAY: Investigating Competing Historical Arguments

To create history, historians generally move from query to judgment. Specifically, they investigate primary sources for clues about life in the past, and after evaluating and organizing these clues, they offer a judgment of what life in the past was like. When working in the field of historiography, however, historians investigate as their primary sources the interpretative judgments of previous historians to find insights about the life and times of these historians. A central purpose of the "What Others Say" section is to help students learn how to identify similarities and differences between various historical interpretations, and to establish meaningful associations between these varying interpretations and the life experiences of the historians who rendered them.

Below are a dozen succinct statements about the nature or purpose of history that have been attributed to a sample of influential historians, philosophers, and literary figures that have contributed to the development of Western thought. The comments are listed according to the chronological year of birth of these authors.

Read and reflect on the judgments expressed in these comments by rearranging their statements into any non-chronological grouping that interests you. For example, you could choose to divide the authors into those you have heard about and those you have not heard about; into those with whom you agree and disagree, or into those you understand and those you do not.

After further reflection, select at least three figures that you would like to learn more about, and conduct secondary source research to find information about their lives and times. As you learn more about them, restate in your own words the meaning of their quotes regarding history. Can you find any connections between the ideas each author expresses and his/her times and/or life experiences?

Document 1: Selected Quotes – Historians on History

> The study of history is the best medicine for a sick mind; for in history you have a record of the infinite variety of human experience plainly set out for all to see; and in that record you can find yourself and your country both examples and warnings; fine things to take as models, base things rotten through and through, to avoid.
> Livy (64 or 59 BCE – 17 CE)

> Whoever wishes to foresee the future must consult the past; for human events ever resemble those of preceding times. This arises from the fact that they are produced by men who ever have been, and ever shall be,

animated by the same passions, and thus they necessarily have the same results.
Niccoló Machiavelli (1469 – 1527)

History consists, for the greater part, of the miseries brought upon the world by pride, ambition, avarice, revenge, lust, sedition, hypocrisy, ungoverned zeal, and all the train of disorderly appetite.
Edmund Burke (1729 – 1797)

Universal history, the history of what man has accomplished in this world, is at bottom the History of the Great Men who have worked here.
Thomas Carlyle (1795 – 1881)

To history has been assigned the office of judging the past, of instructing the present for the benefit of future generations. This work does not have such a lofty ambition. It wants only to show what actually happened.
Leopold von Ranke (1795 – 1886)

History has now been for the first time systematically considered, and has been found, like other phenomena, subject to invariable laws.
August Comte (1798 – 1857)

My object…has been simply to show our causes for national shame in the manner of our treatment of the Indians. It is a shame which the American nation ought not to lie under, for the American people, as a people, are not at heart unjust.
Helen Hunt Jackson (1830 – 1885)

It is the business of the historian to generalize and to guess as to the cause and effect, but he should do it modestly and not call it 'science,' and he should not regard it as his first duty, which is to tell the story.
George Macaulay Trevelyan (1876 – 1962)

History is too much about wars; biography too much about great men.
Virginia Woolf (1882 – 1941)

History is, in its essentials, the science of change. It knows and it teaches that it is impossible to find two events that are ever exactly alike, because the conditions from which they spring are never identical.
Marc Bloch (1886 – 1944)

Study the historian before you begin to study the facts.... By and large, the historian will get the kind of facts he wants. History means interpretation.
E. H. Carr (1892 – 1982)

The writing of history reflects the interests, predilections, and even prejudices of a given generation.
John Hope Franklin (1915 – 2009)

LOOKING BACKWARD/LOOKING FORWARD: Thinking Historically

An Oral History Project:

In one hundred words or less, describe your sentiments toward history. Then conduct an oral interview with an acquaintance or relative, preferably a generation or two older than you, and capture in a few words her/his appreciation for the study of the past. Compare the two accounts, and construct a compelling argument that offers an explanation for the similarities and/or differences in these accounts.

A Project Based Learning Assignment:

Gather with a group of your classmates who completed the "What Others Say" exercise, and ascertain biographical information (author's field of specialty, nationality, ethnicity, gender, and any other characteristic of interest) on each of the 12 authors. Reflect on your findings. What associations do you find to be noteworthy? What are some possible explanations for these associations? Based on the information your group collects, draft some tentative statements about the practice of history, and then critique each statement. What additional research could be undertaken to test the validity of your hypotheses?

SUGGESTED READINGS

A classic and useful work about history and the historical method is Carl G. Gustavson's *A Preface to History* (McGraw-Hill, 1959). For a more recent study, see John H. Arnold's *History: A Very Short Introduction* (Oxford University Press, 2000). For students interested in currents in historiography, see Norman J Wilson's *History in Crisis?*

Recent Directions in Historiography (Prentice Hall, 1999) and Mark Gilderhus's *History and Historians* (Pearson, 2010). For an excellent guide to writing and formatting, we recommend *A Manual for Writers of Research Papers, Theses, and Dissertations* that is published by the University of Chicago Press. Because formatting and citation rules are continuously under revision, be sure that you consult the most recent edition of this work.

ONLINE RESOURCES

The World According to Herodotus
http://upload.wikimedia.org/wikipedia/commons/0/05/Herodotus_World_Map.jpg

Primary Sources
The Histories of Herodotus
http://classics.mit.edu/Herodotus/history.html

A PREMISE AND A CHALLENGE

In summary, both the structure and content of this textbook supports the same end: to transform students into historians. The mantra of this text is *"create history, don't memorize it."*

If you are still not persuaded that:

> *historians exist not to memorize and regurgitate the past, but to create "history",*
>
> *the primary objective of history survey courses is NOT to teach students everything they need to know about history, but to help them become historians; and*
>
> *American historians understand that stories of the past include complex and fascinating tales of intrigue, adventure, irony, and fulfilled and unfulfilled dreams that offer insight into why Americans think and behave as they do,*

then we challenge you to keep an open mind as you read the following pages. Allow us an opportunity to present our case to you.

At the end of the semester, no matter what opinions you hold, we encourage you to send to us on the Green Publishing House website your thoughts about history in general and about this textbook in particular. Did reading this text change your attitude about history? Did it help you to become a better historian? Specifically, what pieces of the text did you find to be most and least helpful? What changes would you recommend in future editions? What other days in history should be included in order to revise and finish this work?

The insights you provide will be helpful to both future students and to the authors of this text. And for those who offer constructive criticism, do not be surprised if the next edition of this textbook incorporates some of your ideas.

Chapter 5:
Defining the American Dream, July 2, 1776
The Declaration of Independence & the Forging of a New Nation

PRELUDE

At the top of the mountain, drops of water form at the edge of the melting snow. The drops gather into a bubble for a while until the pull of gravity breaks them away. The water's unwritten goal is to find a path that leads to the ocean. What path will this journey take? It's impossible to predict. As the trickle of water flows down the mountainside, it encounters barriers – perhaps twigs or rocks. It turns right or left, or backs up for a while. Momentum builds and the stream grows into a river, pushing past trees, perhaps spilling over a cliff to form a waterfall. In time, the power of this flow carves its own path. Its course becomes more predictable and steady, but it is still not unchangeable. Even the path of an immense river can be changed by the convulsions of an earthquake.

The United States was once much like the trickle of water on the mountainside. Its beginnings were fragile. Yet even in its infancy it aspired to lofty goals. Thomas Jefferson articulated such aspirations in the Declaration of Independence, stating that "all men are created equal," and that government exists to secure the God-given rights to "Life, Liberty, and the pursuit of Happiness." Four score and seven years later, Abraham Lincoln restated these goals, reminding his fellow Americans that the nation "was conceived in liberty and dedicated to the proposition that all men are created equal."

Since its founding, the United States, like that pristine drop of water destined for the ocean, has been moving on an epic journey in search of a grand end. The gravitational pull that has guided America's past has been the quest to secure liberty and establish equality for all of its peoples. Of course, the ongoing pursuit of liberty and equality is not the only theme in American history, but it is a motif that has shaped the contours of the American past. This goal has never been fully achieved, but every generation has embraced it as the centerpiece of the American creed.

CONCEIVED IN LIBERTY – THE STORY BEHIND THE STORY

The story of the dramatic birth of the United States is the focus of this chapter. Birth, however, is the consequence of conception, not conception itself. Before a nation can be born, first an idea of nationhood must form in the minds of the people, and be taken full term. Before there could be an American nation, there first had to be Americans united behind a common purpose. What were the grand ideas that unified Americans and prompted them to announce the birth of a new nation?

Late in life, an elderly John Adams spoke to these questions when he reflected on the momentous times in which he lived. "What do we mean by the American Revolution?" he asked.

> Do we mean the American War? The Revolution was effected before the War commenced. The Revolution was in the Minds and Hearts of the People. A Change in their Religious Sentiments of their Duties and Obligations.

Adams understood that a radical change in the people's understanding of their sacred duties and obligations had taken place before the war for independence. The story of this change in "the Minds and Hearts of the People" is the story behind the story of the creation of the United States. It is the story of the birth of the American.

Describing this nebulous revolution in the hearts and minds of the people is a challenging task. Late 18th century colonists, like Americans today, were ideologically, politically, and socially diverse. By the end of the colonial period, however, the supporters of the American Revolution stood united behind one common proposition: coercive civil authority comes only from voluntary consent, and exists for the sole purpose of promoting the security, welfare, or happiness of the people. Whatever other sentiments coalesced to create America, this nation was founded on a commitment to this grand idea.

This particular point of view regarding the origins and purposes of legitimate government has a rich history. Although it was "self-evident" to 18th century Americans, this idea was not self-evident to the ancient Greek philosophers. Both Plato and Aristotle viewed government as natural and ever present in society, and thus, spoke about government's proper forms and aims, but paid scant attention to its origins.

The early Christians also were not unanimous in their interpretations of the claims of government. Orthodox Christians acknowledged God to be the source of government, and advocated obedience to those whom God placed in authority, but whether obedience was demanded to all rulers or only to just rulers was a unresolved question that was debated by churchmen across the centuries. Some early church fathers like Saint Gregory and, at times, Saint Augustine suggested that unqualified obedience to rulers was the Christian norm. From the ninth century onward, however, most Christian thinkers rejected the idea of unqualified obedience, and insisted that governments were created by consent and had to meet a moral test before they could claim legitimate coercive powers over the people.

Educated 18th century American elites were aware of the subtleties of this theological debate. They particularly were influenced by the political theories of the Protestant Reformers. John Calvin taught that God ordained government but allowed humans to select its form; Theodore Beze asserted that the people had a moral duty to resist evil rulers; and Johannes Althusius and John Milton insisted that sovereignty rested with the people who had the power to choose and depose rulers.

The American colonists also were influenced by the theories on government promoted by 17th century British social philosophers like John Locke. According to Locke, individuals in a state of nature voluntarily consented to become a part of a community under one government, which thereafter was empowered to act in the name of the people until it violated the contract of original consent.

From the arguments of these theologians and social philosophers, more and more colonists came to embrace the libertarian creed that God had empowered the people, first, to select the form of government that seemed most likely to procure their happiness, and second, to maintain the right to judge the performance of that government.

But what constitutes a people? The idea of consent always assumes a community— a unified body that shares a set of common beliefs. At what point did the colonists come to see themselves as a distinct people who were unified by adherence to some basic beliefs?

From the earliest accounts of colonization, it is clear that the original English colonists who settled North America viewed themselves not as Americans, but as English men and women who lived in America. As generations passed, and as growing numbers of Germans, Africans, Scots-Irish and other ethnic groups arrived, thus making the population of North America less English and more cosmopolitan, more and more colonists began to envision themselves as part of a distinct community of Americans.

As we discussed in Chapter 4 of Volume 1, the shift from European to American became more pronounced during the middle decades of the century as a consequence of two historic events - the Great Awakening and England's colonial wars against France and Spain. Here is a brief synopsis of that discussion.

The Great Awakening, a religious revival that rippled throughout the thirteen English colonies during the middle decades of the century, was spurred by the thunderous oratory of traveling preachers who spoke not simply from the pulpits of church houses, but from makeshift platforms that were erected in parks and town squares. The most famous of these traveling preachers was George Whitefield, an Anglican minister who on one occasion preached in the Boston Commons to some 23,000 religious seekers, or at least curiosity seekers. Since the population of Boston at this time was only 13,000, this single event attracted an audience almost twice the size of America's third largest city. In many ways, these religious gatherings were the 18th century equivalents to modern day media events such as the Super Bowl and rock festivals. The spontaneity and down-to-earth preaching of these revivals stood in marked contrast to more traditional worship styles typified by etiquette and convention.

The revivals attracted great media attention, in part because of their size, and in part because they provided a rare opportunity for large and socially mixed crowds to gather and intermingle. Before the 1740s, newspapers in the colonies reported primarily European news. During the Great Awakening, however, colonial newspapers reported details of the traveling evangelist's preaching tours and detailed the controversies that followed their revivals. For the first time, colonists from Massachusetts were reading about events that were happening in Georgia. Suddenly, there were new and growing communication lines springing up that connected colonists across the various regions.

As America's first truly mass movement, the Great Awakening was instrumental in persuading thousands of colonists that it was more important to obey one's conscience than to submit to the authority of ordained ministers. This concept reinforced the growing belief that rebellion could be justified when the cause was noble. The controversies surrounding the revivals also forced many commoners to reflect upon theories long pondered by the educated elites: what is the source of legitimate authority, and under what conditions is resistance to it morally justified?

The second noteworthy mid-century event that brought greater unity to the colonies was the seemingly never-ending conflict between England and her perennial enemies, France and Spain. Between 1739 and 1748, first skirmishes with Spain (known as the War of Jenkin's Era) and later the War of Austrian Succession (known in England as "King George's War") pitted the British against the French, Spanish and Prussians. To help the motherland, in 1745 American colonists attacked and conquered the French fortress Louisbourg in Nova Scotia, a victory that was reported with great pride in colonial newspapers. When the war-ending Treaty of Aix-la-

Chapelle of 1748 made "status quo ante bellum" (meaning there would be no territorial exchanges because of military actions during the war) the premise of the peace settlement, these same colonial newspapers reported with equal ferocity the disappointing and shocking news that the fortress won with American blood had to be given back to the despised French.

Unsurprisingly, the treaty that ended the War of Spanish Succession did not resolve the disputes between the French Canadians and the British Americans since both parties still held claim to the Ohio River Valley, a region that also was the tribal land of different groups of Native American peoples whose survival often depended on betting correctly on which European invader with whom to establish trading and diplomatic ties. Within a few years after the Peace of 1748, English population expansion into this region—movements that threatened existing French-Indian fur trade networks—triggered the outbreak of the French and Indian War, an American conflict that soon escalated into the global Seven Years' War (1756-1763).

This world war, like the previous one that pitted the European powers and their colonies against each, produced far-reaching unintended consequences. For instance, during the early years of the conflict when the British military command treated American intelligence and militias with disdain, the colonies contributed little to the British war efforts, thus securing the scorn of Crown officials. Correspondingly, during this time the British suffered frequent military setbacks, thereby reminding the colonists that the British military machine was anything but invincible. Although the tide of the war turned more favorably for the British after William Pitt—a friend of the colonists—assumed wartime leadership and issued orders that the America militias be treated as equal partners, the emerging rift between the British high command and the Americans left hard feelings that neither side was quick to forgive. The war, thus, soured Crown-colonies' relations for years to come, and left the colonists with more confidence in themselves and less in the ability of Great Britain's imperial leadership to effectively control events in America.

After decades of on-and-off fighting, the seemingly never-ending wars for empire finally ended in 1763 with a decisive British victory over its French rival. In the Treaty of Paris of 1763, Britain ousted France from North America, thus formally ending, at least for the moment, French ambitions on the continent. As a consequence of the treaty, the British Empire in America doubled its pre-war size.

Unfortunately, this victory came at a heavy price.

For example, the victory over the French generated a series of English-Indian conflicts as native groups, upset at the defeat of their French allies, organized to resist the encroachment of British settlers onto their ancestral tribal lands. Historians generically refer to these conflicts as Pontiac's Conspiracy, a term named after the Ottawa leader Pontiac who played a prominent role in fomenting this Native American rebellion.

Pontiac's war erupted in 1763 when Native Americans, dismayed that the British under governor-general Jeffrey Amherst refused to honor the French practice of presenting annual supplies to the tribes, attacked and destroyed a number of British settlements in the region surrounding the Great Lakes. The resulting war, though brief, was vicious as both sides resorted to brutal tactics that included the targeting of civilians, the execution of prisoners, and in the case of the British who dispersed smallpox-infested blankets to Native Americans with the intent of spreading the disease, the use of biological warfare.

Even before the outbreak of Pontiac's rebellion, British advisors to King George III were at work developing a policy designed to reduce tensions between Native American tribes and the Crown by creating a boundary line—known as the Proclamation Line of 1763—that theoretically would prevent future hostilities by separating British settlers from Native American peoples. This policy announced that all land with rivers that flowed into the Atlantic Ocean would be reserved for British settlers, while all land with rivers that flowed into the Mississippi River would remain off-limits, at least temporarily, to colonial expansion. This proclamation also prohibited private purchases of tribal lands, essentially giving the Crown, not the colonies, a monopoly on all future western land purchases.

Most colonists grew to despise the Proclamation Line, as did most Native Americans after it proved ineffective in stopping the influx of English settlement across the Appalachian Mountains. Although George III did not create this policy in reaction to the Native American revolt of 1763, these near simultaneous events—Pontiac's Conspiracy and the Proclamation Line of 1763 exposed and exacerbated tensions between the inhabitants of North America and a British Empire that was determined to assert greater authority over this region.

Another adverse outcome of the Seven Years' War was that its heavy costs burdened Britain with a massive war debt that could not be ignored. In response to the postwar financial crisis, the British government decided that the Americans must shoulder a greater share of the financial burdens caused by expenses of the colonial wars. To the British, such expectations seemed entirely reasonable. To the Americans, however, Great Britain's efforts to restrict the colonists' economic freedoms not only drained potential wealth from America, but also encroached on basic liberties that the English tradition granted to all British subjects, no matter where they lived. Despite Britain's military victory in the Seven Years' War, governing the fruits of that victory would prove to be a difficult chore.

THE LONG ROAD TO REBELLION

In 1763, George Grenville became Britain's prime minister. Unlike his brother-in-law William Pitt, Grenville believed that the American colonies had too long been coddled and that a no-nonsense policy with the colonies was long overdue. Specifically, he wanted the Navigation Acts that regulated trade throughout the empire to be rigorously enforced in America. To do this, he advocated issuing general search and seize warrants that did not expire that would allow British custom officials to search anywhere at any time for any illegally smuggled good without having to obtain a specific warrant. Grenville also wanted to establish a permanent military force of 10,000 troops that would be stationed in America, presumably to protect the colonies from Indian uprisings such as Pontiac's Conspiracy. To help pay for this protection, he also wanted to raise revenue in the colonies through parliamentary taxation. None of these objectives would find much support among colonists who disliked

Britain's regulatory acts of trade, viewed peacetime armies as an encroachment against the liberties of British peoples, and believed that taxation without consent of the people violated British cherished traditions.

Under Grenville's leadership, in 1764 the British Parliament passed the Sugar Act, which taxed sugar sold in the colonies. Although the tax was "indirect," (meaning that it was paid by British merchants who imported the sugar and not American consumers), the tax still raised the price of sugar goods, including the price of rum, which was the favorite alcoholic beverage in the northern colonies. Some colonists considered the act unfair and even suggested that the colonists protest by refusing to import these British goods.

In 1765 Parliament conceived of another way to make money from the colonies. It passed the Stamp Act – a "direct tax" on newspapers, almanacs, pamphlets, broadsides, legal documents, dice, and playing cards. This act was even more offensive to the colonists since it was the first time that Parliament assessed a tax that was paid directly by American consumers.

In response to the Stamp Act, colonists protested by creating a secret organization, the "Sons of Liberty," to harass the appointed stamp agents, and by calling a Stamp Act Congress. In October 1765, twenty-seven delegates representing nine of the thirteen colonies issued protests declaring that Americans were equal to all other British subjects and should not be taxed without representation. This Congress also encouraged Americans to refuse to buy any goods from England until Parliament repealed this unjust tax. When British merchants began suffering the effects of the American boycott, they complained to members of Parliament. As a result, in 1766 Parliament repealed the Stamp Act, although it also passed a Declaratory Act stating that it could continue to make laws that were binding on the colonies.

With the repeal of the Stamp Act, relations between the colonists and mother England temporarily improved. However, when Parliament at the urging of the chancellor of the Exchequer Charles Townshend reenacted indirect taxes on selected imported goods such as glass, paper, lead and tea, Americans again organized protests against this "British tyranny." Unsurprisingly, these protests eventually led to bloodshed.

On March 5, 1770, a rally in Boston against British troops stationed in this city erupted in name-calling, then physical confrontation. The mob grew until it was out of control. Finally, British soldiers fired on the civilians. The first to die (and the first martyr in the cause of the American Revolution) was Crispus Attucks, a fugitive slave who had escaped from his master and had worked for twenty years as a merchant seaman. In all, five men were killed. The news was quickly reported to the colonists by the use of color engravings printed and distributed by Paul Revere. Throughout the colonies this event became known as the Boston Massacre.

After this disaster, cooler heads prevailed, and England removed the indirect taxes on glass, paper and lead. Parliament, however, insisted on maintaining the tax on tea, not so much to raise revenue from the colonies, as to defend the principle of its right to tax. As a result, a minority of Americans continued their protest, refusing to purchase British tea.

When the American boycott of tea brought the British East India Tea Company to the brink of bankruptcy, in 1773 the British Parliament passed the Tea Act, a law that gave economic benefits to the company without eliminating the small colonial tax on tea. This action further angered the Americans. As a result, on December 16, 1773, a group of Boston patriots dressed as Indians protested the tax on tea by dumping 342 crates of tea in the harbor — an action known as the "Boston Tea Party."

This protest quickly escalated tension between Parliament and the colonists. The British passed a series of acts to punish the colonists for their destruction of property and disrespect for British law. To the Americans, these "Coercive acts" were "intolerable." In response to this crisis, in 1774 the Americans called a Continental Congress to discuss what action could be taken. Twelve of the thirteen colonies (all except Georgia) sent delegates to this Philadelphia gathering.

At this meeting, the Americans sent strongly worded messages to Parliament and King George III demanding that the "Intolerable Acts" be rescinded. The Americans gave the British until May 1775 to respond to their ultimatum. At that time, the delegates declared that they would return to Philadelphia to determine their next recourse. Meanwhile, a total boycott of trade with England would be strictly enforced.

Between the meetings of the First and the Second Continental Congress, British troops continued their attempts to quell the American protests. On April 19, 1775, when General Thomas Gage, British Military Governor of Massachusetts, sent a garrison to seize arms and ammunition at Concord, a rebel band of "minutemen" confronted the British on a bridge near Lexington. The resulting battle left dead and wounded on both sides. It was the first instance of British casualties and foreshadowed events to come.

After the colonial delegates returned to Philadelphia, the Continental Congress officially created the Continental Army and asked George Washington to serve as the Commander in Chief. Yet, even in the midst of growing conflict, many delegates continued to seek a peaceful resolution with King George III. On July 5, 1775, Congress sent an "Olive Branch Petition" to the Crown, seeking reconciliation against further hostilities. The King, however, rejected the petition and declared that Americans "were engaged in open and avowed rebellion." Tensions worsened when Americans learned that the King had hired German mercenaries to stop the American rebellion. The Continental Congress responded by creating an American Navy and began a search for foreign assistance.

Meanwhile, citizens throughout the colonies debated the goals of the crusade against British tyranny. To Thomas Paine, fighting simply to restore harmonious relations with the motherland made no sense. In January 1776, Paine published an argument for independence in an electrifying fifty-five-page masterpiece entitled *Common Sense*. Written in a plain style that Americans of all classes could understand, *Common Sense* was an instant hit, selling 120,000 copies in three months. Paine's pamphlet helped transform reluctant rebels into republican revolutionaries.

In April 1776, North Carolina empowered its delegates to the Continental Congress to support "independency." A month later, Virginia issued a similar proclamation, and on June 7, 1776, Richard Henry Lee first introduced his fateful resolution calling for a complete separation from English rule. The controversial measure, however, did not pass on that day.

Hoping that a delay would produce a more unified front, Congress recessed for three weeks. At the same time, it appointed a Committee of Five to draw up a statement presenting the case for independence. This Committee selected the talented thirty-three year old Thomas Jefferson to write a first draft of this statement. While many of the other delegates were away from the city, Jefferson remained in Philadelphia, created a rough draft of this document and then gave it to Benjamin Franklin and John Adams to edit. By the end of June, the Committee had completed its work. If and when Congress decided to act on the Virginia resolution, a document that articulated the reasons for independence would be ready.

Yet even after Congress reconvened on July 1, 1776, it was still unclear whether the delegates would approve this formal and final break with the motherland. Tension over the Virginia resolution filled the statehouse. When a delegate from Pennsylvania attempted to delay the decision, John Adams responded with a fervent plea to take immediate action. At that time it was clear that nine colonies favored independence, but two colonies (Pennsylvania and South Carolina) opposed it. In addition, the delegation from Delaware was split, and the New York delegates refused to vote until they received further instructions from home. With a solid but a non-unanimous majority in favor of independence, Congress decided to defer the decision one more day.

For most Americans the idea of revolution, which seemed so improbable just a year earlier, was now in everyone's mind and heart. The delegates were well aware that Britain was a formidable power and not easily challenged. Yet here in Philadelphia in July 1776, these patriots were on the brink of a critical decision, a vote away from initiating the birth of a new nation.

PAUSE-REFLECT-THINK

Thirteen years had passed since the British Crown attempted to assert greater control over the colonies following the conclusion of the Seven Years' War. Six years had passed since American colonists were gunned down by British soldiers during the Boston Massacre. Fifteen months had passed since American Minutemen exchanged fire with British Redcoats at the Battle of Lexington. And yet, the colonists were still fighting, not for independence from Britain, but to be granted the same rights that Britain granted all of its subjects, no matter where they lived.

How do you explain the hesitation and the divided loyalties of the colonists in July 1776? If you were a delegate in Philadelphia on that occasion, how would you have cast your vote, and why?

THE BIG EVENT
DECISION TIME, JULY 2, 1776

A time for decision had come. The small gathering of patriots — some would call them traitors — faced a momentous decision. With deathly certainty they knew what would happen if they acted boldly and their revolution failed. Less predictable was what would happen if it actually succeeded. Only the most visionary could have imagined that the decision made on this day would trigger changes that would ripple down through the centuries to produce the most diverse and powerful country the world had ever known.

On July 2, 1776, representatives from the thirteen colonies prepared to vote on a resolution declaring American independence from Britain. As delegates entered the hall and took their seats, no one could predict the outcome of the impending vote. If even a single colony vehemently objected to the resolution, Congress threatened to postpone declaring independence. While most colonies supported the resolution, the Delaware representatives disagreed on the measure — one delegate in favor and one opposed. The decision depended on Delaware's third delegate, Caesar Rodney, who favored independence. Trapped in a raging thunderstorm somewhere between Dover and Philadelphia, he waited for a break in the storm.

The resolution before Congress, proposed by Virginia delegate Richard Henry Lee, boldly stated an act of treason against the British King:

> Resolved: That these United Colonies are, and of right ought to be, free and independent States, that they are absolved from all allegiance to the British Crown, and that all political connection between them and the State of Great Britain is, and ought to be, totally dissolved.

What could possibly persuade the Continental Congress delegates to risk their lives and fortunes on a favorable vote for Lee's resolution? These reasonable and educated patriots knew that previous uprisings by other colonies against British rule brought violence but little lasting reform. Why should they expect this revolution, their revolution, to be any different? They also knew that their action today would face certain failure unless the colonies stood united in the cause. Therefore, a critical question faced them on this day: would Congress support Lee's proposal *without* opposition?

Between sundown July 1 and sunup July 2, intense pressure convinced most of the wavering delegates to join the cause. The delegates from South Carolina agreed for the sake of unity to support independence. Meanwhile, two Pennsylvania delegates opposed to the resolution (John Dickinson and Robert Morris) agreed to abstain so that the majority of the Pennsylvania delegation would be in favor of independence.

The elimination of the only remaining opposing vote hinged on Caesar Rodney's arrival to sway Delaware's delegation toward independence. The meeting began with Rodney still missing. Fortunately, before Delaware's turn to vote, Rodney arrived at the state house, wet from head to foot from riding his horse through the rain. He broke the tie, and the Delaware delegation voted "yea." Lee's resolution to declare independence from Great Britain passed unanimously. (New York abstained while waiting the approval from its own state legislature.)

Now that the delegates had committed themselves to the idea of unified rebellion, work began immediately to finalize the wording of the declaration that would announce their intentions to the world. The following day, John Adams wrote to his wife Abigail:

> The Second Day of July, 1776 will be the most memorable Epoch in the History of America....It ought to be solemnized with Pomp and Parade, Shows, Games, Sports, Guns, Bells, Bonfires, and Illuminations from one end of the Continent to the other from this Time forward forevermore.

But the date remembered as America's official birthday came two days later, after Jefferson's "Declaration of Independence" had been debated, revised, and ultimately accepted. The final document, less idealistic than Jefferson's original intention, contained several compromises to appease certain colonies. These compromises would haunt Americans for centuries to come. Among the revisions approved during these days of debate included the elimination of a paragraph that denounced the evils of slavery and blamed the perpetuation of this institution on England's King George III. "He [George III] has waged cruel war against human nature itself," Jefferson originally had written,

> violating its most sacred rights to life and liberty in the persons of distant people who never offended him, captivating and carrying them into slavery in another hemisphere, or to

incur miserable death in their transportation thither.

Southern voices at this time were unwilling to accept this direct anti-slavery rhetoric, and thus they eliminated this passage, although paradoxically they were willing to embrace the ideals encompassed in the opening section of the Declaration of Independence:

> We hold these truths to be self-evident: that all men are created equal, that they are endowed by their Creator with certain unalienable rights, that among these are life, liberty, and the pursuit of happiness....

The meaning of the statement "all *men* are created equal" has been debated by Americans almost since the day this visionary ideal was first ratified. In fact, about seven decades later, about a hundred women and a few men would gather in Seneca Falls, New York, to produce a document designed to promote the ideal of sexual equality. Using the Declaration of Independence as their model, the authors of this "Declaration of Rights and Sentiments" eliminated the ambiguity present in Jefferson's original Declaration of Independence, unequivocally asserting that "all men and women are created equal."

If this interpretation of the phrase was not in the minds of all of the men who signed the Declaration, the ideal of sexual equality was in the minds of some of their spouses. Three months before the approval of the Declaration, Abigail Adams lobbied for American women when she penned these words to her husband John Adams:

> I long to hear that you have declared an independency–and by the way in the new Code of Laws which I suppose it will be necessary for you to make I desire you would Remember the Ladies, and be more generous and favorable to them than your ancestors. Do not put such unlimited power into the hands of the Husbands. Remember all Men would be tyrants if they could. If particular care and attention is not paid to the Ladies we are determined to foment a Rebellion, and will not hold ourselves bound by any Law in which we have no voice, or Representation.

Although Abigail Adams's particular concerns would not be addressed by the delegates to the Second Continental Congress (either in the Declaration of Independence or in the first constitution, the Articles of Confederation, which they subsequently would write), the concept of equality for all has been a part of the American political vision since before the birth of the nation.

In the late afternoon of July 4, President of the Congress John Hancock announced the adoption of the historic document, which asserted that when people are exposed to a long series of "abuses and usurpations" they have the right to "throw off such Government, and to provide new Guards for their future security." Later Congress ordered that "the Declaration passed on the 4th, be fairly engrossed on parchment ... and ... be signed by every member of Congress." A month after Congress declared Independence, members of Congress present in Philadelphia signed the prepared parchment. Hancock signed first, with a signature large enough to be read by King George without the need of eye glasses. Over the next several weeks, a few members not present on August 2 added their signatures to the document.

Because the composition of Congress changed slightly during the month after the declaration, and because some delegates who originally were unwilling to support independence (e.g., Robert Morris) changed their positions after the declaration, while others who were not present in July (e.g., Richard Henry Lee) later signed the document, the fifty-six signatures on this cherished document are not identical to the individuals who voted for independence in early July. All of these "signers" were white adult men between the ages of twenty-six and seventy-five. Eight were born in England, Scotland or Ireland, but most were American-born. By profession, a majority were practicing lawyers, although the group also included four physicians and two clergy. The wealthiest of the signers was the only Roman Catholic in the group, Charles Carroll of Maryland.

For almost two and one half centuries, this historic document has expressed ideals that have defined for many what often has been referred to as the American dream. The Declaration of Independence declares that people are "created equal" and should therefore have equal and fair treatment under the law. It proclaims that Americans are not subjects of any foreign power, but are citizens of a free land. These ideals, although not originally applied to slaves, women and other minority groups, nevertheless contained timeless truths that have inspired freedom-loving peoples from around the world for more than two centuries.

POSTLUDE

IMPLEMENTING THE AMERICAN DREAM

With the great American experiment now begun, two major challenges lay ahead. First, a war against a more powerful foe had to be won. Second, this new unproven and untested republican concept of government had to succeed. Meeting either challenge would be difficult.

Declaring independence, thus, announced the ending of an era of colonial dependency, but it did not end the battle for freedom. Instead, it set in motion an entire new series of events. Tough and critical years lay ahead. No longer could great masses of Americans hold a neutral opinion on the war. Most Americans quickly joined the crusade for independence, although a significant minority (perhaps as many as one in four) remained loyal to the Crown. During the ensuing war years, states routinely confiscated the property of these "Loyalists" to fund the revolution. As a result, many Loyalists—perhaps more than 100,000—fled into Canada.

Declaring independence also had international, strategically important consequences. As long as America continued its attempts to restore harmony with the British Empire, foreign powers refused to offer support. After the Declaration, however, England's perennial foes eagerly came to America's side.

In 1778, France signed an alliance with the United States, promising not to end the conflict until Britain acknowledged America's independence. The next year, Spain declared war on Britain, and the following year Holland entered the war. Even the neutral nations of Europe ganged up against Britain. Catherine the Great of Russia attempted to take advantage of Britain's vulnerability by persuading Denmark-Norway, Sweden, the Holy Roman Empire, Prussia, and Portugal to join Russia in forming an Armed Neutrality to demand changes in international law that the British had long opposed. In short, the American Revolution soon became more than a family-squabble between the British and the Americans; rather, it pitted Britain against a generally hostile world.

In 1782, the British relented and sought to end the war with only minor losses. To Britain, this meant accepting losses to the upstart Americans, but not to its perennial rivals. Britain secretly approached Benjamin Franklin, the U.S. ambassador to Europe, with an offer. Although the Alliance of 1778 with France prohibited separate peace settlements, Franklin agreed to negotiate with the British in secret, correctly realizing that U.S. leverage would be greater without France and Spain being involved in the settlement. After initializing a tentative agreement with Britain, Franklin then had to inform the French what he had done. Amazingly, his tactful diplomacy convinced the French to accept his settlement with grace.

The Treaty of Paris, formally signed in 1783 by all the warring parties, gave the United States what it wanted. In the settlement, the British recognized the independence of the United States and granted to it all land south of Canada, north of Florida, and east of the Mississippi River. Spain received

Florida. The British also agreed to remove its troops from American soil without destroying property, a euphemism for not freeing the slaves. In return, the United States agreed to ask the states to return confiscated land back to the Loyalists and not to pass laws placing legal impediments preventing British creditors from collecting their pre-war debts.

Winning both the war and the peace were impressive accomplishments, but even these achievements did not guarantee national survival, much less the implementation of the lofty ideals embraced in the Declaration of Independence. At this time the supreme law of the United States was known as the Articles of Confederation. Drafted in 1777 by the same Continental Congress that embraced the Declaration of Independence, this constitution created a "league of friendship" among the thirteen states. Under the Articles, each state retained its sovereignty, but also sent representatives to a national Congress with limited powers over the states. These included the power to declare war, maintain an army and navy, conduct foreign affairs, deliver the mail, and arbitrate disputes between the sovereign states.

At this time the United States government had no executive branch or national court. To further ensure its weakness, it lacked the authority to tax the people or to regulate interstate trade. Although consistent with the views of those who signed the Declaration of Independence, to some the self-designed constitutional weaknesses in the new United States government threatened the success of the American experiment. To these Americans more worried about security than liberty, unless a second political revolution took place, the revolutionary dreams of the patriots could become simply a footnote in world history.

THE CRITICAL PERIOD – THE ECONOMY OF IMPOTENCE

During and immediately after the Revolutionary War, the American economy suffered devastating setbacks. Under the system of British mercantilism, almost all of the clients with whom Americans traded were British subjects. Although independence provided Americans with the freedom to negotiate trading agreements with the peoples of nations that permitted open trade, it also severed their business ties with most of their former trading partners. Without trading privileges with the British, everyone knew that the infant nation would temporarily suffer from economic hardships. The question of whether the nation would be able to survive until new commercial relationships could be established haunted American business leaders during these bleak days of transition.

In difficult economic times, individual states attempted to protect themselves by imposing tariffs on goods coming in from other states. Without overseas trading outlets and with tariff barriers stifling interstate trade, commercial activities slowed, causing severe deflation, which in turn produced devastating consequences for debtors. By 1787, prices plunged to 50% of what they were just six years earlier. Repaying debts with such a deflated currency proved to be impossible for large numbers of Americans, including that body of workers notoriously in debt – American farmers. Unable to meet their mortgage obligations, thousands of farmers lost their lands, and with their lands, they lost their means of existence.

As frustration turned into anger, some resorted to radical actions. In Rhode Island, debtors persuaded the state assembly to order the printing of inflated currency. Bankers fled the state and literally went into hiding so not to be paid in this legal, yet worthless currency. In Massachusetts, 1500 indebted rebels led by the former Revolutionary War hero Daniel Shays freed imprisoned debtors from the jails and used physical force and intimidation to prevent the courts from foreclosing on mortgages. Such actions of political irresponsibility and even mob violence convinced many that something had to be done to deal with the economic crisis.

Without the constitutional authority to regulate trade, or even to prohibit state tariffs or the printing of state currencies, some members of Congress desired to strengthen the national government through constitutional amendments. In February 1787, Congress reluctantly asked the states to send delegates to a convention in Philadelphia "for the sole and express purpose of revising the Articles of Confederation." To legally alter the Articles, all thirteen states would have to agree on the recommended changes. Ultimately, twelve states sent delegates to Philadelphia; Rhode Island, however, refused to participate.

AMERICA REINVENTS ITSELF

Between May and September 1787, fifty-five delegates from twelve states gathered at Independence Hall, Philadelphia. Early in the proceedings they decided to close the deliberations to the public. To ensure candor, nothing discussed on the floor of Independence Hall would be announced to the public until after their work had been completed. Having thus secured secrecy, they made their second great decision. Notwithstanding their Congressional mandate to "revise" the Articles, this new convention decided to tear up the current constitution and start afresh on a completely new constitution.

The delegates that gathered in Independence Hall in 1787 were not the same group that had declared independence eleven years earlier. Of the fifty-odd signers of the Declaration of Independence, only five (Benjamin Franklin, Roger Sherman, Robert Morris, George Clymer and James Wilson) would sign the Constitution of 1787.

Among the patriots of 1776 not present at the Convention of 1787 were Richard Henry Lee (the man who introduced the Virginia Resolution), John Adams (the delegate who seconded the independence motion), Thomas Jefferson (the author of the Declaration of Independence), John Hancock (the President of the Continental Congress), Charles Thomson (the Secretary of the Continental Congress), and Samuel Adams (the patriotic fireball largely responsible for the opening shots of the American Revolution).

Some of these missing political leaders, like Jefferson who was the U.S. Minister to France, and Adams, who was the U.S. Minister to Britain, could not attend because they were out of the country. Among these, Adams supported the proceedings in Philadelphia; Jefferson expressed ambivalence. Other revolutionary leaders, like Virginia's Patrick Henry— perhaps best known today for his famous "Give me liberty or give me death" speech—refused to attend, stating bluntly that he "smelled a rat."

During the summer of 1787, the founders who gathered at Philadelphia produced a document that opened with these well-known words:

> We the People of the United States, in Order to form a more perfect Union, establish Justice, insure domestic Tranquility, provide for the common defence, promote the general Welfare, and secure the Blessings of Liberty to ourselves and our Posterity, do ordain and establish this Constitution for the United States of America.

PAUSE-REFLECT-THINK

In the summer of 1787, would you have supported the ratification of the new constitution?

Not all Americans greeted this new constitution with enthusiasm.

Patriots such as Richard Henry Lee and Patrick Henry distrusted it because, according to them, the Constitution of 1787 recreated a type of authoritarian government alarmingly similar to the one that the freedom fighters overthrew in the revolution. Indeed, the Constitution of 1787 provided for the creation of a President with kingly powers, a national court that took from Congress the power to settle interstate disputes, and a bi-cameral Congress with extensive powers, including the authority to regulate trade and to tax. Equally important, the new constitution extended the term lengths and eliminated the term-limit restrictions that the Articles had placed upon members of Congress. It eliminated the rights of the states to coin money and to keep ships of war, and it included no Bill of Rights to protect designated individual liberties such as the freedom of assembly, freedom of speech, and freedom of the press.

Moreover, unlike the Declaration of Independence or the Articles of Confederation, the Constitution of 1787 was alarmingly secular, making no reference to God or to the "Great Governor of the World." It even included provisions for a federal census, which the biblically literate recognized as one of the great sins of Israel during the reign of King David. Finally, according to the opponents, the Constitution of 1787 dangerously threatened the liberties won in the revolution and violated the original constitution, since it declared that the new government would take effect whenever nine (not thirteen) states approved it.

For each challenge, however, the supporters of the Constitution of 1787 provided a defense and an explanation. In essence, these "Federalists" argued that the new document, although imperfect, better enabled the government to solve the nation's ills than the impotent Articles of Confederation. Moreover, owing to the more reasonable amendment process contained in the new constitution, the Constitution of 1787 allowed the new nation both to confront its immediate problems and to make future adjustments that enabled the nation to respond to later concerns. To the Federalists, the authors of the Constitution at Philadelphia had carefully created a system that balanced the national twin concerns for liberty and security. To these Americans, the ratification of the Constitution of 1787 provided the only way to ensure that future generations would enjoy the unalienable rights to "life, liberty and the pursuit of happiness."

Ultimately, the arguments of George Washington, James Madison, Alexander Hamilton, John Jay and the other Federalists won the day. On June 21, 1788, when New Hampshire became the ninth state to grant its approval, the Constitution of 1787 replaced the Articles of Confederation as the supreme law of the land and became the basis for the United States government we know today. Within a year, twenty-six state-appointed Senators and sixty-four newly elected Congressmen watched George Washington take a presidential oath to uphold the Constitution of the United States. The era of Federalism had arrived. The name of the nation — the United States— was finally on its way to becoming a singular noun.

PROBING THE SOURCES: Three Revolutionary Visions: *Common Sense*, The Declaration of Independence, and the Constitution of 1787

Presented below are selections from three historic documents that express the ideals of a revolutionary generation of American founders. To what degree are these revolutionary visions similar and different? What type of American would have supported or opposed each of these visions, and why?

Document 1: Excerpts from Thomas Paine, *Common Sense* (1776)

Thomas Paine published anonymously this fiery political pamphlet in January 1776 at a time when many Americans were first beginning to debate the advisability of independence. Few books, if any, have had as large a percentage of Americans discuss its merits. How do you explain the popularity of this piece?

> SOME writers have so confounded society with government, as to leave little or no distinction between them; whereas they are not only different, but have different origins.

Society is produced by our wants, and government by our wickedness; the former promotes our happiness POSITIVELY by uniting our affections, the latter NEGATIVELY by restraining our vices. The one encourages intercourse, the other creates distinctions. The first is a patron, the last a punisher.

Society in every state is a blessing, but Government, even in its best state, is but a necessary evil; in its worst state an intolerable one: for when we suffer, or are exposed to the same miseries BY A GOVERNMENT, which we might expect in a country WITHOUT GOVERNMENT, our calamity is heightened by reflecting that we furnish the means by which we suffer. Government, like dress, is the badge of lost innocence; the palaces of kings are built upon the ruins of the bowers of paradise. For were the impulses of conscience clear, uniform and irresistibly obeyed, man would need no other lawgiver; but that not being the case, he finds it necessary to surrender up a part of his property to furnish means for the protection of the rest; and this he is induced to do by the same prudence which in every other case advises him, out of two evils to choose the least. Wherefore, security being the true design and end of government, it unanswerably follows that whatever form thereof appears most likely to ensure it to us, with the least expense and greatest benefit, is preferable to all others. ...

Small islands not capable of protecting themselves, are the proper objects for kingdoms to take under their care; but there is something very absurd, in supposing a continent to be perpetually governed by an island. In no instance hath nature made the satellite larger than its primary planet, and as England and America, with respect to each other, reverses the common order of nature, it is evident they belong to different systems: England to Europe, America to itself....

Ye that tell us of harmony and reconciliation, can ye restore to us the time that is past? Can ye give to prostitution its former innocence? Neither can ye reconcile Britain and America. The last cord now is broken, the people of England are presenting addresses against us. There are injuries which nature cannot forgive; she would cease to be nature if she did. As well can the lover forgive the ravisher of his mistress, as the continent forgive the murders of Britain. The Almighty hath implanted in us these unextinguishable feelings for good and wise purposes. They are the guardians of his image in our hearts. They distinguish us from the herd of common animals. The social compact would dissolve, and justice be extirpated from the earth, or have only a casual existence were we callous to the touches of affection. The robber, and the murderer, would often escape unpunished, did not the injuries which our tempers sustain, provoke us into justice.

  O ye that love mankind! Ye that dare oppose, not only the tyranny, but the tyrant, stand forth! Every spot of the old world is overrun with oppression. Freedom hath been hunted round the globe. Asia, and Africa, have long expelled her. — Europe regards her like a stranger, and England hath given her warning to depart. O! receive the fugitive, and prepare in time an asylum for mankind.

Document 2: Comparative drafts of the Declaration of Independence (1776)

Although it is not possible to reconstruct with complete confidence the stages of the drafts of the Declaration, printed below is a close reconstruction of Jefferson's original draft as it stands in comparison with the version of the Declaration of Independence that Congress ultimately approved. The ~~struck through~~ words represent portions of Jefferson's original draft that were edited or eliminated by Congress while the **[bolded and bracketed]** words represent additions Congress made to Jefferson's original version. What significant differences do you find in these drafts?

[To reduce confusion in the reading of this document, a larger font and different margins are being used.]

~~A Declaration by the Representatives of the UNITED STATES OF AMERICA, in General Congress Assembled~~ **[The unanimous declaration of the thirteen United States of America in Congress, July 4, 1776]**

When, in the course of human events, it becomes necessary for ~~a~~ **[one]** people to ~~advance from that subordination in which they have~~

~~hitherto remained~~ [**dissolve the Political Bands which have connected them with another**], & [**and**] to assume among the powers of the earth, the ~~equal and independent~~ [**separate and equal**] station to which the laws of nature & [**and**] of nature's ~~god~~ [**God**] entitle them, a decent respect to the opinions of mankind requires that they should declare the causes which impel them to the ~~change~~ [**separation**].

We hold these truths to be ~~sacred & undeniable~~ [**self-evident**], that all men are created equal ~~& independent~~; that ~~from that equal creation they derive in rights inherent & inalienables, among which are the preservation of~~ [**they are endowed, by the CREATOR, with certain inalienable rights, that among these are**] life, & liberty & [**and**] the pursuit of happiness; that to secure these ~~ends~~ [**rights**], governments are instituted among men, deriving their just powers from the consent of the governed; that whenever any form of government shall become destructive of these ends, it is the right of the people to alter or to abolish it, &

[and] to institute new government, laying its foundation on such principles and organizing it's powers in such form, as to them shall seem most likely to effect their safety & [and] happiness. prudence, indeed, will dictate that governments long established should not be changed for light & [and] transient causes: and accordingly all experience hath shewn that mankind are more disposed to suffer while evils are sufferable, than to right themselves by abolishing the forms to which they are accustomed. but when a long train of abuses & [and] usurpations, ~~begun at a distinguished period, &~~ pursuing invariably the same object, evinces a design to ~~subject~~ [reduce] them ~~to arbitrary power under absolute despotism~~, it is their right, it is their duty, to throw off such government, & [and] to provide new guards for their future security. such has been the patient sufferance of these colonies; & [and] such is now the necessity which constrains them to expunge their former systems of government. the history of his present ~~majesty~~ [King of Great Britain] is a history of

~~unremitting~~ [**repeated**] injuries and usurpations, ~~among which no fact stands single or solitary to contradict the uniform tenor of the rest~~, all ~~of which have~~ [**having**] in direct object the establishment of an absolute tyranny over these states. to prove this, let facts be submitted to a candid world~~,~~ [.] ~~for the truth of which we pledge a faith yet unsullied by falsehood.~~

~~he~~ [**He**] has refused his assent to laws, the most wholesome and necessary for the public good:

~~he~~ [**He**] has forbidden his governors to pass laws of immediate ~~&~~ [**and**] pressing importance, unless suspended in their operation till his assent should be obtained; and when so suspended, he has neglected utterly to attend to them.

~~he~~ [**He**] has refused to pass other laws for the accommodation of large districts of people unless those people would relinquish the right of representation [**in the legislature**], a right inestimable to them ~~&~~ [**and**] formidable to tyrants ~~alone~~ [**only**]:

[**He has called together legislative bodies at places unusual, uncomfortable, and distant** from the depository of their public Records, for the sole purpose of fatiguing them into compliance with his measures.]

~~he~~ [He] has dissolved representative houses repeatedly ~~& continually~~, for opposing with manly firmness his invasions on the rights of the people.

~~he~~ [He] has refused for a long ~~space of~~ time, [after such Dissolutions,]to cause others to be elected, whereby the legislative powers, incapable of annihilation, have returned to the people at large for their exercise, the state remaining in the meantime exposed to all the dangers of invasion from without, and convulsions within:

~~he~~ [He] has endeavored to prevent the population of these states; for that purpose obstructing the laws for naturalization of foreigners; refusing to pass others to encourage their migration hither, ~~&~~ [and] raising the conditions of new appropriations of lands:

~~he~~ [He] has ~~suffered~~ [obstructed] the administration of justice ~~totally to cease in some~~

~~of these colonies~~, [by] refusing his assent to laws for establishing judiciary powers:

~~he~~ [He] has made our judges dependent on his will alone, for the tenure of their offices, and [the] amount of their salaries.

~~he~~ [He] has erected a multitude of new offices ~~by a self-assumed power~~, ~~&~~ [and] sent hither swarms of [new] officers to harrass our people, ~~&~~ [and] eat out their substance.

~~he~~ [He] has kept among us, in times of peace, standing armies ~~& ships of war:~~ [**without the Consent of our Legislatures.**]

~~he~~ [He] has affected to render the military, independent of ~~&~~ [and] superior to civil power:

~~he~~ [He] has combined with others to subject us to a jurisdiction foreign to our ~~constitutions~~ [**Constitution**], and unacknowledged by our laws; giving his assent to their pretended acts of legislation,

~~for~~ [For] quartering large bodies of armed troops among us;

~~for~~ [For] protecting them, by a mock trial, from punishment for any murders [**which**] they should commit on the inhabitants of these states;

~~for~~ [For] cutting off our trade with all parts of the world;

~~for~~ [For] imposing taxes on us without our consent;

~~for~~ [For] depriving us [**, in many cases,**] of the benefits of trial by jury;

~~for~~ [For] transporting us beyond seas to be tried for pretended offenses;

[**For abolishing the free System of English Laws in a neighbouring Province, establishing therein an Arbitrary government, and enlarging its Boundaries so as to render it at once an example and fit instrument for introducing the same absolute rule into these Colonies**:]

~~for~~ [For] taking away our charters [**, abolishing our most valuable Laws**], ~~&~~ [**and**] altering fundamentally the forms of our governments;

~~for~~ **[For]** suspending our own legislatures, ~~&~~ **[and]** declaring themselves invested with power to legislate for us in all cases whatsoever;

~~he~~ **[He]** has abdicated government here, **[by declaring us out of his Protection, and waging War against us]** ~~withdrawing his governors, & declaring us out of his allegiance and protection~~;

~~he~~ **[He]** has plundered our seas, ravaged our coasts, burnt our towns, ~~&~~ **[and]** destroyed the lives of our people:

~~he~~ **[He]** is at this time transporting large armies of foreign mercenaries to compleat the works of death, desolation ~~&~~ **[and]** tyranny, already begun with circumstances of cruelty ~~&~~ **[and]** perfidy **[scarcely paralleled in the most barbarous age, and totally]** unworthy the head of a civilized nation:

[He has constrained our fellow Citizens taken Captive on the high Seas to bear Arms against their Country, to become the executioners of their friends and brethren, or to fall themselves by their hands.]

~~he~~ **[He]** has **[excited domestic insurrections amongst us, and has]** endeavored to bring on the inhabitants of our frontiers the merciless Indian savages, whose known rule of warfare is an undistinguished destruction of all ages, sexes and conditions ~~of existence~~:

~~he has incited treasonable insurrections of our fellow citizens with the allurements of forfeiture & confiscation of our property:~~

~~he has waged cruel war against human nature itself, violating it's most sacred rights of life & liberty in the persons of a distant people who never offended him, captivating & carrying them into slavery in another hemispere, or to incure miserable death in their transportation hither. this piratical warfare, the opprobium of *infidel* powers, is the warfare of the *Christian* king of Great Britain. determined to keep open a market where MEN should be bought and sold, he has prostituted his negative for suppressing every legislative attempt to prohibit or to restrain this execrable commerce and that this assemblage of horrors might want no fact of distinguished die,~~

~~he is now exciting those very people to rise in arms among us, and to purchase that liberty of which~~ *~~he~~* ~~had deprived them, by murdering the people upon whom~~ *~~he~~* ~~also obtruded them: thus paying off former crimes committed against the~~ *~~liberties~~* ~~of one people, with crimes which he urges them to commit against the~~ *~~lives~~* ~~of another.~~

In every stage of these oppressions we have petitioned for redress in the most humble terms: our repeated petitions have been answered only by repeated injury. a prince, whose character is thus marked by every act which may define a tyrant, is unfit to be the ruler of a **[free]** people **[.]** ~~who mean to be free. future ages will scarce believe that the hardiness of one man, adventured within the short compass of twelve years only, on so many acts of tyranny without a mask, over a people fostered and fixed in principles of liberty~~.

Nor have we been wanting in attention to our British brethren. ~~we~~ **[We]** have warned them from time to time of attempts by their legislature to extend an unwarrantable jurisdiction over

~~these our states~~ [**us**]. ~~we~~ [**We**] have reminded them of the circumstances of our emigration ~~&~~ [**and**] settlement here, ~~no one of which could warrant so strange a pretension: that these were effected at the expence of our own blood & treasure, unassisted by the wealth or the strength of Great Britain: that in constituting indeed our several forms of government, we had adopted one common king, thereby laying a foundation for perpetual league & amity with them: but that submission to their parliament was no part of our constitution, nor ever in idea, if history may be credited: and we~~ [**We have**] appealed to their native justice ~~&~~ [**and**] magnanimity, ~~as well as~~ [**and we have conjured them**] to the ties of our common kindred to disavow these usurpations, which ~~were likely to~~ [**would inevitably**] interrupt our ~~correspondence & connections~~ [**Connexions and Correspondence**]. ~~they~~ [**They**] too have been deaf to the voice of justice ~~&~~ [**and**] of consanguinity, ~~& when occasions have been given them, by the regular course of their laws, of removing from their councils the disturbers of~~

our harmony, they have by their free election re-established them in power. at this very time too they are permitting their chief magistrate to send over not only soldiers of our common blood, but Scotch and foreign mercenaries to invade & deluge us in blood. these facts have given the last stab to agonizing affection, and manly spirit bids us to renounce forever these unfeeling brethren, we **[We]** must [, **therefore, acquiesce in the necessity, which denounces our separaton and]** endeavor to forget our former love for them, and hold them, as we hold the rest of mankind, enemies in war, in peace friends. we might have been a free & a great people together; but a communication of grandeur & of freedom it seems is below their dignity. be it so, since they will have it: the road to glory & happiness is open to us too; we will climb it in a seperate state, and acquiesce in the necessity which pronounces our everlasting Adieu!

We **[,]** therefore **[,]** the representatives of the United States of America, in General Congress assembled, [**appealing to the Supreme Judge of**

the World for the Rectitude of our Intentions] do , in the name, ~~&~~ **[and]** by the authority of the good people of these ~~states~~ **[colonies]**, **[solemnly Publish and Declare]** ~~reject and renounce all allegiance & subjection to the kinds of Great Britain & all others who may hereafter claim by, through, or under them; we utterly dissolve & break off all political connection which may have heretofore subsisted between us & the people or parliament of Great Britain; and finally we do assert and declare~~ **[that]** these **[United]** colonies **[are, and of Right ought]** to be free and independent states~~,~~**[:that they are absolved from all allegiance to the British crown, and that all political connection between them and the state of Great Britain is, and ought to be, totally dissolved; and]** that as free ~~&~~ **[and]** independent states they ~~shall hereafter~~ have **[full]** power to levy war, conclude peace, contract alliances, establish commerce, ~~&~~ **[and]** to do all other acts and things which independent states may of right do. And for the support of this declaration, **[with a firm Reliance on the**

Protection of DIVINE PROVIDENCE] we mutually pledge to each other our lives, our fortunes and our sacred honor.

Document 3: Excerpts from the Constitution of 1787 (1787)

Printed below are the Preamble and Article I of the Constitution of 1787. What major issues and concerns are addressed in these sections? To what degree did the founders embrace democracy and/or principles of republican rule?

We the People of the United States, in Order to form a more perfect Union, establish Justice, insure domestic Tranquility, provide for the common defence, promote the general Welfare, and secure the Blessings of Liberty to ourselves and our Posterity, do ordain and establish this Constitution for the United States of America.

Article I

Section 1

All legislative Powers herein granted shall be vested in a Congress of the United

States, which shall consist of a Senate and House of Representatives.

Section 2

1: The House of Representatives shall be composed of Members chosen every second Year by the People of the several States, and the Electors in each State shall have the Qualifications requisite for Electors of the most numerous Branch of the State Legislature.

2: No Person shall be a Representative who shall not have attained to the Age of twenty five Years, and been seven Years a Citizen of the United States, and who shall not, when elected, be an Inhabitant of that State in which he shall be chosen.

3: Representatives and direct Taxes shall be apportioned among the several States which may be included within this Union, according to their respective Numbers, which shall be determined by adding to the whole Number of free Persons, including those bound to Service for a Term of Years, and excluding Indians not taxed, three fifths of all other Persons. The actual Enumeration shall be made within three Years after the first Meeting of the Congress of the United States, and within every subsequent Term of ten Years, in such Manner as they shall by Law direct. The Number of Representatives shall not exceed one for every thirty Thousand, but each State shall have at Least one Representative; and until such enumeration shall be made, the State of New Hampshire shall be entitled to chuse three, Massachusetts eight, Rhode-Island and Providence Plantations one, Connecticut five, New-York six, New Jersey four, Pennsylvania eight, Delaware one, Maryland six, Virginia ten, North Carolina five, South Carolina five, and Georgia three.

4: When vacancies happen in the Representation from any State, the Executive Authority thereof shall issue Writs of Election to fill such Vacancies.

5: The House of Representatives shall chuse their Speaker and other Officers; and shall have the sole Power of Impeachment.

Section 3

1: The Senate of the United States shall be composed of two Senators from each State, chosen by the Legislature thereof, for six Years; and each Senator shall have one Vote.

2: Immediately after they shall be assembled in Consequence of the first Election, they shall be divided as equally as may be into three Classes. The Seats of the Senators of the first Class shall be vacated at the Expiration of the second Year, of the second Class at the Expiration of the fourth Year, and of the third Class at the Expiration of the sixth Year, so that one third may be chosen every second Year; and if Vacancies happen by Resignation, or otherwise, during the Recess of the Legislature of any State, the Executive thereof may make temporary Appointments until the next Meeting of the Legislature, which shall then fill such Vacancies.

3: No Person shall be a Senator who shall not have attained to the Age of thirty Years, and been nine Years a Citizen of the United States, and who shall not, when elected, be an Inhabitant of that State for which he shall be chosen.

4: The Vice President of the United States shall be President of the Senate, but shall have no Vote, unless they be equally divided.

5: The Senate shall chuse their other Officers, and also a President pro tempore, in the Absence of the Vice President, or when he shall exercise the Office of President of the United States.

6: The Senate shall have the sole Power to try all Impeachments. When sitting for that Purpose, they shall be on Oath or Affirmation. When the President of the United States is tried, the Chief Justice shall preside: And no Person shall be convicted without the Concurrence of two thirds of the Members present.

7: Judgment in Cases of impeachment shall not extend further than to removal from Office, and disqualification to hold and enjoy any Office of honor, Trust or Profit under the United States: but the Party convicted shall nevertheless be liable and subject to

Indictment, Trial, Judgment and Punishment, according to Law.

Section 4

1: The Times, Places and Manner of holding Elections for Senators and Representatives, shall be prescribed in each State by the Legislature thereof; but the Congress may at any time by Law make or alter such Regulations, except as to the Places of chusing Senators.

2: The Congress shall assemble at least once in every Year, and such Meeting shall be on the first Monday in December, unless they shall by Law appoint a different Day.

Section 5

1: Each House shall be the Judge of the Elections, Returns and Qualifications of its own Members, and a Majority of each shall constitute a Quorum to do Business; but a smaller Number may adjourn from day to day, and may be authorized to compel the Attendance of absent Members, in such

Manner, and under such Penalties as each House may provide.

2: Each House may determine the Rules of its Proceedings, punish its Members for disorderly Behaviour, and, with the Concurrence of two thirds, expel a Member.

3: Each House shall keep a Journal of its Proceedings, and from time to time publish the same, excepting such Parts as may in their Judgment require Secrecy; and the Yeas and Nays of the Members of either House on any question shall, at the Desire of one fifth of those Present, be entered on the Journal.

4: Neither House, during the Session of Congress, shall, without the Consent of the other, adjourn for more than three days, nor to any other Place than that in which the two Houses shall be sitting.

Section 6

1: The Senators and Representatives shall receive a Compensation for their Services, to be ascertained by Law, and paid out of the Treasury of the United States.6 They shall in all Cases, except Treason, Felony and Breach of the Peace, be privileged from Arrest during their Attendance at the Session of their respective Houses, and in going to and returning from the same; and for any Speech or Debate in either House, they shall not be questioned in any other Place.

2: No Senator or Representative shall, during the Time for which he was elected, be appointed to any civil Office under the Authority of the United States, which shall have been created, or the Emoluments whereof shall have been increased during such time; and no Person holding any Office under the United States, shall be a Member of either House during his Continuance in Office.

Section 7

1: All Bills for raising Revenue shall originate in the House of Representatives; but the Senate may propose or concur with Amendments as on other Bills.

2: Every Bill which shall have passed the House of Representatives and the Senate, shall, before it become a Law, be presented to the President of the United States; If he approve he shall sign it, but if not he shall return it, with his Objections to that House in which it shall have originated, who shall enter the Objections at large on their Journal, and proceed to reconsider it. If after such Reconsideration two thirds of that House shall agree to pass the Bill, it shall be sent, together with the Objections, to the other House, by which it shall likewise be reconsidered, and if approved by two thirds of that House, it shall become a Law. But in all such Cases the Votes of both Houses shall be determined by yeas and Nays, and the Names of the Persons voting for and against the Bill shall be entered on the Journal of each House respectively. If any Bill shall not be returned by the President within ten Days (Sundays excepted) after it shall have been presented to him, the Same shall be a Law, in like Manner as if he had signed it, unless the Congress by their Adjournment prevent its Return, in which Case it shall not be a Law.

3: Every Order, Resolution, or Vote to which the Concurrence of the Senate and House of Representatives may be necessary (except on a question of Adjournment) shall be presented to the President of the United States; and before the Same shall take Effect, shall be approved by him, or being disapproved by him, shall be repassed by two thirds of the Senate and House of Representatives, according to the Rules and Limitations prescribed in the Case of a Bill.

Section 8

1: The Congress shall have Power To lay and collect Taxes, Duties, Imposts and Excises, to pay the Debts and provide for the common Defence and general Welfare of the United States; but all Duties, Imposts and Excises shall be uniform throughout the United States;

2: To borrow Money on the credit of the United States;

3: To regulate Commerce with foreign Nations, and among the several States, and with the Indian Tribes;

4: To establish an uniform Rule of Naturalization, and uniform Laws on the subject of Bankruptcies throughout the United States;

5: To coin Money, regulate the Value thereof, and of foreign Coin, and fix the Standard of Weights and Measures;

6: To provide for the Punishment of counterfeiting the Securities and current Coin of the United States;

7: To establish Post Offices and post Roads;

8: To promote the Progress of Science and useful Arts, by securing for limited Times to Authors and Inventors the exclusive Right to their respective Writings and Discoveries;

9: To constitute Tribunals inferior to the supreme Court;

10: To define and punish Piracies and Felonies committed on the high Seas, and Offences against the Law of Nations;

11: To declare War, grant Letters of Marque and Reprisal, and make Rules concerning Captures on Land and Water;

12: To raise and support Armies, but no Appropriation of Money to that Use shall be for a longer Term than two Years;

13: To provide and maintain a Navy;

14: To make Rules for the Government and Regulation of the land and naval Forces;

15: To provide for calling forth the Militia to execute the Laws of the Union, suppress Insurrections and repel Invasions;

16: To provide for organizing, arming, and disciplining, the Militia, and for governing such Part of them as may be employed in the Service of the United States, reserving to the States respectively, the Appointment of the Officers, and the Authority of training the Militia according to the discipline prescribed by Congress;

17: To exercise exclusive Legislation in all Cases whatsoever, over such District (not exceeding ten Miles square) as may, by Cession of particular States, and the Acceptance of Congress, become the Seat of the Government of the United States, and to exercise like Authority over all Places purchased by the Consent of the Legislature of the State in which the Same shall be, for the Erection of Forts, Magazines, Arsenals, dock-Yards, and other needful Buildings;—And

18: To make all Laws which shall be necessary and proper for carrying into Execution the foregoing Powers, and all other Powers vested by this Constitution in the Government of the United States, or in any Department or Officer thereof.

Section 9

1: The Migration or Importation of such Persons as any of the States now existing shall think proper to admit, shall not be prohibited by the Congress prior to the Year one thousand eight hundred and eight, but a Tax or duty may be imposed on such Importation, not exceeding ten dollars for each Person.

2: The Privilege of the Writ of Habeas Corpus shall not be suspended, unless when in Cases of Rebellion or Invasion the public Safety may require it.

3: No Bill of Attainder or ex post facto Law shall be passed.

4: No Capitation, or other direct, Tax shall be laid, unless in Proportion to the Census or Enumeration herein before directed to be taken.

5: No Tax or Duty shall be laid on Articles exported from any State.

6: No Preference shall be given by any Regulation of Commerce or Revenue to the Ports of one State over those of another: nor shall Vessels bound to, or from, one State, be obliged to enter, clear, or pay Duties in another.

7: No Money shall be drawn from the Treasury, but in Consequence of Appropriations made by Law; and a regular Statement and Account of the Receipts and Expenditures of all public Money shall be published from time to time.

8: No Title of Nobility shall be granted by the United States: And no Person holding any Office of Profit or Trust under them, shall, without the Consent of the Congress, accept of any present, Emolument, Office, or Title, of any kind whatever, from any King, Prince, or foreign State.

Section 10

1: No State shall enter into any Treaty, Alliance, or Confederation; grant Letters of Marque and Reprisal; coin Money; emit Bills of Credit; make any Thing but gold and silver Coin a Tender in Payment of Debts; pass any Bill of Attainder, ex post facto Law, or Law impairing the Obligation of Contracts, or grant any Title of Nobility.

2: No State shall, without the Consent of the Congress, lay any Imposts or Duties on Imports or Exports, except what may be absolutely necessary for executing it's inspection Laws: and the net Produce of all Duties and Imposts, laid by any State on Imports or Exports, shall be for the Use of the Treasury of the United States; and all such Laws shall be subject to the Revision and Control of the Congress.

3: No State shall, without the Consent of Congress, lay any Duty of Tonnage, keep Troops, or Ships of War in time of Peace, enter into any Agreement or Compact with another State, or with a foreign Power, or engage in War, unless actually invaded, or in such imminent Danger as will not admit of delay.

WHAT OTHERS SAY: Remembering the Declaration of Independence

The following documents illustrate some ways that activists, politicians and historians have made use of and interpreted the meaning of the Declaration of Independence.

The first document is taken from the Declaration of Rights and Sentiments, which was mostly written by Elizabeth Cady Stanton and signed in 1848 by about one hundred women and men who attended the first women's rights convention in Seneca Falls, New York.

The second piece is an excerpt from the 1852 Fourth of July speech of Frederick Douglas, a powerful and distinguished 19th century African American social reformer. The third document is the well-known address that President Lincoln delivered in 1863 at the dedication of a soldiers' cemetery in Gettysburg, Pennsylvania.

The final two documents are excerpts from the works of two contemporary distinguished historians, Pauline Maier and David Armitage, who examine, respectively, how the Declaration has come to be revered as a "sacred text" and as a global document.

Document 1: Excerpts from the "Declaration of Rights and Sentiments" (1848)

When, in the course of human events, it becomes necessary for one portion of the family of man to assume among the people of the earth a position different from that which they have hitherto occupied, but one to which the laws of nature and of nature's God entitle them, a decent respect to the opinions of mankind requires that they should declare the causes that impel them to such a course.

We hold these truths to be self-evident: that all men and women are created equal; that they are endowed by their Creator with certain inalienable rights; that among these are life, liberty, and the pursuit of happiness; that to secure these rights governments are instituted, deriving their just powers from the consent of the governed. Whenever any form of government becomes destructive of these ends, it is the right of those who suffer from it to refuse allegiance to it, and to insist upon the institution of a new government, laying its foundation on such principles, and organizing its powers in such form, as to them shall seem most likely to effect their safety and happiness. Prudence indeed, will dictate that governments long established should not be changed for light and transient causes and accordingly all experience hath shown that mankind are more disposed to suffer, while evils are sufferable, than to right themselves by abolishing the forms to which they were accustomed. But when a long train of abuses and usurpations, pursuing invariably the same object evinces a design to reduce them under absolute despotism, it is their duty to throw off such government, and to provide new guards for their future security. Such has been the patient sufferance of the women under this government, and such is now the necessity which constrains them to demand the equal station to which they are entitled.

The history of mankind is a history of repeated injuries and usurpations on the part of man toward woman, having in direct object the establishment of an absolute tyranny over her.

To prove this, let facts be submitted to a candid world.

Document 2: Excerpts from Frederick Douglas, "What to a Slave is the Fourth of July?" (1852)

Fellow citizens, pardon me, and allow me to ask, why am I called upon to speak here today? What have I or those I represent to do with your national independence? Are the great principles of political freedom and of natural justice, embodied in that Declaration of Independence, extended to us? And am I, therefore, called upon to bring our humble offering to the national altar, and to confess the benefits, and express devout gratitude for the blessings resulting from your independence to us? ....

Fellow citizens, above your national, tumultuous joy, I hear the mournful wail of millions, whose chains, heavy and grievous yesterday, are today rendered more intolerable by the jubilant shouts that reach them. If I do forget, if I do not remember those bleeding children of sorrow this day, "may my right hand forget her cunning, and may my tongue cleave to the roof of my mouth!" ....

What to the American slave is your Fourth of July? I answer, a day that reveals to him more than all other days of the year, the gross injustice and cruelty to which he is the constant victim. To him your celebration is a sham; your boasted liberty an unholy license; your national greatness, swelling vanity; your sounds of rejoicing are empty and heartless; your shouts of liberty and equality, hollow mock; your prayers and hymns, your sermons and thanksgivings, with all your religious parade and solemnity, are to him mere bombast, fraud, deception, impiety, and hypocrisy - a thin veil to cover up crimes which would disgrace a nation of savages. There is not a nation of the earth guilty of practices more shocking and bloody than are the people of these United States at this very hour.

Go search where you will, roam through all the monarchies and despotisms of the Old World, travel through South America, search out every abuse and when you have found the last, lay your facts by the side of the everyday practices of this nation, and you will say with me that, for revolting barbarity and shameless hypocrisy, America reigns without a rival.

Document 3: Abraham Lincoln, "The Gettysburg Address," (1863)

Four score and seven years ago our fathers brought forth, upon this continent, a new nation, conceived in liberty, and dedicated to the proposition that "all men are created equal."

Now we are engaged in a great civil war, testing whether that nation, or any nation so conceived, and so dedicated, can long endure. We are met on a great battle field of that war. We come to dedicate a portion of it, as a final resting place for those who died here, that the nation might live. This we may, in all propriety do.

But, in a larger sense, we can not dedicate – we can not consecrate – we can not hallow, this ground – The brave men, living and dead, who struggled here, have hallowed it, far above our poor power to add or detract. The world will little note, nor long remember what we say here; while it can never forget what they did here.

It is rather for us, the living, we here be dedicated to the great task remaining before us – that, from these honored dead we take increased devotion to that cause for which they here, gave the last full measure of devotion – that we here highly resolve these dead shall not have died in vain; that the nation, shall have a new birth of freedom, and that government of the people, by the people, for the people, shall not perish from the earth.

Document 4: Excerpts from Pauline Maier, *American Scripture: Making the Declaration of Independence* (Alfred A Knopf, 1997), pp xi, xvii-xx

In 1776, the Declaration of Independence was not even copied onto a particularly good sheet of parchment, just an ordinary type of colonial manufacture that could be easily found on sale in Philadelphia...[yet] after a period in which the Declaration of Independence was all but forgotten, it was remade into a sacred text, a statement of basic, enduring truths often described with words borrowed from the vocabulary of religion. ...

How and why did the Declaration of Independence come to assume the role it has assumed in American society – a statement of values that more than any other expresses not why we separated from Britain, and not what we are or have been, but what we ought to be, an inscription of ideals that bind us as a people but have also been at the center of some of the most divisive controversies in our history? ....

A theme that goes throughout the book and can at least be stated simply: the remaking of the Declaration of Independence no less than its original creation was not an individual but a collective act that drew on the words and thoughts of many people...who struggled with the same or closely related problems. The eloquence of Jefferson's and Lincoln's [a reference to the Gettysburg Address] texts depended in part on the resonances they captured, and their messages were convincing because the hearts of their audiences had been... "prepared" to receive it. The act of reinterpreting the Declaration, moreover, did not stop with Lincoln; it goes on today...You, I, and less attentive members of the American public are participants. And the story has a moral.

Document 5: Excerpts from David Armitage, *The Declaration of Independence: A Global History* (Harvard University Press, 2007), pp. 3,6-9, 22-23

The Declaration of Independence may have acquired special significance for Americans, but its power as a symbol was potentially global ... it provided the model for similar documents around the world that asserted the independence of other new states....

[Others have studied] sources for the Declaration's language... how it was drafted, edited, and published...the various European sources for the Declaration's statements concerning natural rights, or the right of revolution, whether in English political thought, Scottish moral theory, or Swiss philosophy... That debate has concentrated mostly on the Declaration's second paragraph and its 'self-evident' truths; it has not been broadened to consider other elements... such as the meaning of the independence it claimed for the United States. Recovering that meaning will be a major concern of this book. ...

Putting American history into global perspective ... can help to show that ... 'globalization' is not a novel condition. ...The generation of Europeans and Americans that came of age in the decades before 1776 was almost the first in human history to have ready access to a comprehensively global vision of their place in the world... a postwar world decisively shaped by imperial rivalry and global competition. ...

This is what the Declaration of Independence declared: that the former United Colonies were now "the United States of America" because they were "free and independent states." No document in world history before 1776 had made such an announcement of statehood in the language of independence. A great many later documents would do just that. Indeed, the global history of the two centuries after 1776 would show that creating the flexible instrument with which others could declare their independence proved to be as momentous an innovation ... as ushering "the United States of America" onto the world stage in July 1776 had been.

LOOKING BACKWARD/LOOKING FORWARD: Who Supports What?

An Assessing Change and Continuity Exercise:

In 500 words or less, address the question: In what ways did the Constitution of 1787 reflect and reject the values contained in the Declaration of Independence? Support your essay with primary source evidence.

A Project Based Learning Assignment: Is All Politics Local?

Gather into a group of students who have completed the above question. As a group, select one of the original thirteen colonies as your focal point, and conduct research to find the demographic and political profiles of the inhabitants of that colony/state in 1776 and in 1787. What portions of the population would have supported and opposed the Declaration of Independence and the Constitution of 1787, and why? Explain these attitudes in each period and compare them with the opinions of inhabitants of colonies/states in other regions. Be able to support your conclusions with primary source evidence. Write an essay or present a lecture that summarizes your arguments.

SUGGESTED READINGS

The classic and still read analyses of the thought contained in the Declaration is Carl Becker's *The Declaration of Independence: A Study in the History of Political Ideas* (New York, Harcourt Brace, 1922). Garry Wills's *Inventing America: Jefferson's Declaration of Independence* (Vantage Books, 1978) challenges Becker's thesis by arguing that the document's philosophy rests more on the Scottish Enlightenment than on the thought of John Locke. For a thorough textual analysis of the document itself, see Julian P. Boyd, *The Declaration of Independence: The Evolution of the*

Text as Shown in Facsimiles of Various Drafts by its Author (Library of Congress, 1943).

In addition to Pauline Maier's *American Scripture: Making the Declaration of Independence* (Alfred A Knopf, 1997) and David Armitage's *The Declaration of Independence: A Global History* (Harvard University Press, 2007)--which are cited in the Probing the Sources section--we recommend Jay Fliegelman's *Declaring Independence: Jefferson, Natural Language, and the Culture of Performance* (Stanford University Press, 1993), a lively, provocative book that argues that the Declaration was written to be spoken as well as read. Students interested in examining how the Declaration has been interpreted across the centuries will enjoy reading the documents in Justin Buckley Dyer's source book, *American Soul: The Contested Legacy of the Declaration of Independence* (Rowman & Littlefield, 2012).

ONLINE RESOURCES

Audios and Videos

Morgan Freeman's short film on the Declaration, released 2002
https://www.youtube.com/watch?v=jYyttEu_NLU

Talking History Audio on life and legacy of Thomas Paine
http://www.oah.org/site/assets/talkinghistory/2006/ThomasPaine-56k.mp3

Illustrations

John Dunlap's July 4, 1776 Broadside
http://lcweb2.loc.gov/cgi-bin/ampage?collId=rbc3&fileName=rbc0001_2004pe76546page.db

John Trumbull's famous painting of signing
http://www.google.com/imgres?imgurl=&imgrefurl=http%3A%2F%2Fen.wikipedia.org%2Fwiki%2FUnited_States_Declaration_of_Independence&h=0&w=0&tbnid=_5hV0cAySB4jZM&zoom=1&tbnh=183&tbnw=276&docid=G7SYjxsjgPcZ7M&tbm=isch&ei=wbEAVIO5OcnHggTxloL4Ag&ved=0CAgQsCUoAg

Maps

Proclamation Line of 1763
http://www.history.com/news/wp-content/uploads/2013/10/proclamation.jpg

Population Density, 1775
http://www.westpoint.edu/history/SiteAssets/SitePages/American%20Revolution/02PopulationDensity.gif

Major Campaigns of the Revolutionary War
http://www.westpoint.edu/history/SiteAssets/SitePages/American%20Revolution/01ARPrincipalCampaigns.gif

John Wallis's Map of the United States at the time of Peace of 1783
http://www.loc.gov/resource/g3700.ct000080/

Visual Primary Sources

Religion and the Congress of the Confederation, 1774 – 1789
http://www.loc.gov/exhibits/religion/rel04.html#obj104

Cartoon: The Cruel Fate of the Loyalists
http://www.loc.gov/pictures/resource/ppmsca.37324/

Chapter 6:

Undeclaring War, February 18, 1799: Navigating Neutrality & the Ramifications of the Pursuit of Peace

PRELUDE

On July 4, 1826, Providence seemed to smile on America. Even as the grandchildren of the revolutionary patriots were celebrating the 50th birthday of their nation, two of the three surviving signers of the Declaration of Independence, Thomas Jefferson and John Adams, died within a few hours of each other. Other than George Washington, no other Americans epitomized the spirit and triumphs of the young nation as much as these two former patriots, statesmen, ambassadors, vice presidents, and presidents. Though different in temperament, religion, and politics, by the golden anniversary of the United States both of these men had long secured a lofty place in the shrines of the Republic that they had helped to establish.

Before their deaths, each of these American giants suggested inscriptions for their tombstones. There is great insight and irony in the words that each man chose for his epitaph. Jefferson, the twice-elected president who is remembered for doubling the size of the United States through the negotiation and purchase of the Louisiana Territory, allowed no words on his tomb except the following:

> author of the Declaration of Independence,
> of the Statute of Virginia for religious freedom,
> and Father of the University of Virginia.

To Jefferson, individual or national greatness was not best measured by position, wealth, or grandeur, but by commitment to the inalienable rights of liberty of conscience. The America with which Jefferson most wanted to be associated was the America that he wanted to build – an America free from tyranny, bigotry, and ignorance.

Similarly, John Adams also expressed in a few words an assessment of his greatest legacy to the nation. On his tombstone, Adams asked that these simple words be inscribed:

> Here lies John Adams,
> who took upon himself the responsibility
> of Peace with France in the year 1800.

That Adams at the end of his extensive public career should desire above everything else to be remembered for avoiding war with France points to the magnitude of the difficult but epoch-making decision that he quietly made from his presidential office on February 18, 1799.

Although this action may be little known even by history buffs, the outcome of this decision not only demonstrated that Adams placed country above both party and career, but also forever changed the course of the nation that Adams so dearly loved. To set the stage for this silent moment of consequence, we first will describe the perilous decade that preceded this nation-altering decision.

WASHINGTON'S BALANCING ACT – LIBERTY & SECURITY IN THE FEDERALIST ERA

Neither Adams nor Jefferson participated in the Philadelphia convention that produced the Constitution of 1787 because as the young nation's leading diplomats, Adams was in London and Jefferson in Paris. From this distance, each looked at the state efforts to ratify the new constitution with interest. Neither thought the new constitution was perfect, with Jefferson fearing it provided too much power to the

President, and Adams, too much power to the Senate. Both were disappointed that it did not contain a bill of rights. Despite his quibbles, Adams strongly urged its ratification because he believed that the nation desperately needed an effective central government led by a powerful president to bring stability to a country currently amuck in inter-state wrangling. Although Jefferson did not campaign against ratification, as an advocate of representative democracy and states' rights, he expressed sympathy to those who opposed the creation of strong central government.

Following the ratification of the Constitution, both men returned from abroad to assume leadership roles in the new government. After the Electoral College selected Washington as President and Adams as Vice President, Washington formed his cabinet, asking Jefferson to serve as Secretary of State and Alexander Hamilton, an "ultra" nationalist (or High Federalist), to serve as Secretary of Treasury. Washington purposefully created a philosophically diversified Cabinet in the hopes of forming a unified government that included individuals who embraced differing opinions regarding the appropriate role of the central government.

Not unexpectedly, Washington's advisers rarely agreed on matters of policy. This division appeared early over an issue, which in hindsight appears trivial, but which at the time was emotionally explosive. Adams, who believed the nation needed a strong executive to protect the nation's interests, urged Congress to confer a "regal" title on the President, such as "His Most Benign Highness" or "His Majesty." Jefferson considered such suggestions ridiculous, stating, "I hope the terms Excellency, Honor, Worship, [and] Esquire forever disappear from among us." On this occasion, Jefferson's opinion won the day as Congress agreed to address the President with the simple salutation, "Mr. President." Over the ensuing years, however, on most matters the President and Congress would align themselves with moderate Federalists like Adams or High Federalists like Hamilton, who favored a more active role of the central government in the life of the nation.

For example, when confronted with the daunting task of finding a solution to the nation's economic crisis, Washington and Congress supported Hamilton's plan to fund at par value the never-paid revolutionary era national debt ($54 million) and to assume the debt of the delinquent states ($21 million) that still had not repaid their revolutionary era obligations. Although Hamilton advocated this in order to re-establish a credit line for the young nation, funding the national and state debts provided a financial boon to those who had speculated in old government bonds, which had often been purchased from their original holders for about thirty cents on the dollar.

To be able to make these payments, Congress also followed Hamilton's advice and enacted an 8% tariff on foreign goods, a tax that provided some protection to American manufacturers even as it brought in revenue. Congress also placed a hefty 25% excise tax on whiskey—a beverage rarely consumed in the North—but the favorite alcoholic drink of Westerners and Southerners. Thus, within a brief time the new government, following the recommendations of Hamilton, had dramatically increased its national debt and raised national taxes in ways that benefited northern manufacturers at the expense of southern and western farmers.

Opposition to the "whiskey tax" was so great on the western frontier that in 1794 Washington felt compelled to call up 13,000 militiamen (a larger force than he ever commanded during the Revolution) to corral the "Whiskey Rebels" who challenged the authority of the federal government to tax distilled spirits. When the 13,000 militiamen marched into western Pennsylvania, however, they met few resisters. Although in many ways a "tempest in a teapot," the crushing of this so-called Whiskey Rebellion was important because it demonstrated Washington's willingness to use military force if necessary to compel obedience to the national government.

The authority of the national government also increased in scope when Washington and Congress accepted Hamilton's recommendation to grant a twenty-year charter for a national bank. The United States government and private investors jointly owned this First Bank of the United States, another boon for wealthy Americans. Since the Constitution of 1787 made no specific provision for such an institution, the creation of this bank sparked considerable controversy. Despite the constitutional objections expressed by Secretary of State Jefferson and others who insisted that the constitution be interpreted strictly, on this issue President Washington agreed with Hamilton and the "loose constructionists" who argued that the "implied powers" of the constitution authorized the creation of a powerful national bank.

Washington's support for Hamilton's economic agenda won applause in some regions and disdain in others. Because the commercial and budding manufacturing states of the North greatly benefited from these initiatives, Hamilton's program was popular in these regions. In the agrarian South and West, however, these programs were grossly unpopular.

By the mid-1790s, opposition to Hamilton's policies became more organized, ultimately resulting in the creation of an emerging political faction to challenge President Washington and the Federalist Party. This growing partisanship in government angered Washington and played a major role in convincing him not to serve as President beyond the completion of his second four-year term.

In time, this emerging party of opposition under the leadership of Jefferson and James Madison would become known as the Democratic Republican Party, or more succinctly, the Republican Party. Although named the Republican Party, this party should not be confused with the later party of Lincoln or the modern day Republican Party. Rather, this southern- and western-based opposition party led by Jefferson and Madison that emphasized individual freedoms, farms over factories, and limited government was the distant relative of the modern-day Democratic Party.

Unlike the Federalists who generally favored rule by the more cultured and educated elites, and who advocated a system that drew the most virtuous men into public life and then insulated them from the necessity of pandering to the unwashed masses, the Republicans of the 1790s were more receptive to the democratic impulses of an age that increasingly questioned deferential politics based upon social distinctions. As proponents of free speech and free press, the Republicans voiced opposition to the growing powers of the central government, including the administration's support for the protective tariff, the whiskey tax, the central bank, and the expansion of the national debt.

Despite Washington's misgivings regarding the rise of an opposition party, most Americans viewed these political developments favorably. For those still fearful of the central government, the emerging two-party system provided a safeguard against the tyranny of single party rule. This liberty-conscious generation also took comfort in the ten amendments added to the Constitution in 1791 when the Bill of Rights was ratified. These amendments enumerated rights not explicitly mentioned in the constitution, including, for instance, the freedom of religion, speech, free press, free assembly, the right to form militias and receive speedy trials before impartial juries, and protections against unreasonable searches and double jeopardy [being charged twice for the same offense]. The Bill of Rights also placed limitations on the power of the central government, reserving some powers to the states and the public. These additions made explicit what the Federalists claimed the Constitution of 1787 always implied, that power should be shared between the national and state government, with neither having the authority to encroach upon the inalienable rights of Americans. According to these Federalists, the ideals of the Declaration of Independence and the provisions of the new U.S. Constitution agreed fully in intent and purpose.

PAUSE – THINK- REFLECT

What form of government is most likely to devise policies that serve the best interests of all of the inhabitants of that society? Should public policy reflect the opinions of all of the inhabitants of a region, or should officials who are the most informed about the issues involved formulate it? Can the will of the majority be trusted to recognize the rights of the minority?

FOREIGN AFFAIRS OF THE FEDERALIST ERA

For several decades following the ratification of the Constitution of 1787, the newly established national government found it easier to "insure domestic tranquility" than to "provide for the common defense." The major superpowers of the world, Britain and France, viewed the infant United States as a political aberration and a second-rate power unworthy of serious attention. Obtaining respect in such an environment proved difficult.

Although Great Britain promised in the Treaty of Paris (1783) to withdraw its troops from American soil, more than a decade would pass before the British Redcoats left the American frontier. Britain also displayed its condescension toward the United States by refusing to grant it a commercial treaty and by refusing to send a diplomatic minister to the upstart nation. When American Congressmen threatened to retaliate by imposing special custom duties on Britain, the British finally relented in 1791 and dispatched their first official diplomat to America. Unbeknownst to the Americans, however, the British minister's secret instructions were to forestall anti-British legislation by pretending to discuss grievances with the Americans without ever conceding anything.

Even as Washington's administration sought international respect from Britain, another crisis erupted in 1793 when the French revolutionary government, after guillotining King Louis XVI, declared war on Great Britain. During the American Revolution, the United States signed a treaty with Louis XVI that pledged eternal friendship with France. After the French executed Louis XVI, however, Washington wondered if the United States was still morally bound to honor this treaty. When he asked his Cabinet for advice, Washington received, not surprisingly, contradictory responses. Jefferson supported the alliance with France; Hamilton opposed it. Ultimately, Washington decided to recognize the French revolutionary government, but also to issue a proclamation of neutrality that declared the intention of the United States to remain at peace. Washington's Proclamation of Neutrality asserted America's intention to trade with both Britain and France, a reasonable policy, but also one replete with dangers.

In 1794, as Americans attempted to trade with the French in the French West Indies, the British Navy began seizing hundreds of American ships. Britain justified these seizures by referring to the so-called Rule of 1756, an international agreement that stated that neutral nations could not trade in times of war where they were not permitted to trade before the war began. The United States, which did not exist in 1756, had never agreed to this principle of international law, and thus protested what it considered to be the illegal British seizures of American ships.

As anti-British sentiment spread across America, Hamilton urged Washington to send a special commissioner to England to settle the brewing conflict. Washington agreed. Bypassing the U.S. State Department, Washington selected the Chief Justice of the Supreme Court and staunch New York Federalist, John Jay, to go to England. Jay's instructions were to demand British indemnities for the seizures of U.S. ships, secure the evacuation of British forces from the American frontier, and obtain a favorable commercial treaty with England without violating the terms of America's Alliance of 1778 with France.

Jay had no chance of securing these demands, particularly since Hamilton weakened his bargaining position by privately informing the British minister in Philadelphia that the United States would never consider going to war against Britain or even aligning itself with nations hostile to the British Empire. In late 1794, Jay returned to the United States with a treaty in hand. Jay's Treaty was not what Washington had ordered, but it was the best that Jay could deliver.

According to the terms of the agreement, Britain again promised (as it did in 1783) to remove its troops from American land, and agreed to grant the United States minimal trading rights with its colonies in the British West Indies. In return, however, the United States agreed to repay all revolutionary era debts still owed to British creditors, and to embrace the principles of the Rule of 1756.

For Republicans back home, this latter agreement was unfair to France and a departure from America's policy of neutrality. Secretary of State Randolph opposed the treaty, as did the U.S. Minister to France James Monroe, but with Washington's support, the Senate ratified it by the narrowest 20-10 margin.

BY-PRODUCTS OF JAY'S TREATY

Jay's Treaty, although unproductive in many ways, provided the United States a few precious achievements. It forestalled war with Britain, resulted in the removal of British troops from the Northwest Territory, and restored minimal and desperately needed trading rights with portions of the British Empire. Moreover, because of the improved relations with Britain that resulted from Jay's Treaty, Spain suddenly recognized the need to make concessions to the United States in order to prevent a possible Anglo-American alliance that potentially could threaten Spanish territory west of the Mississippi River. Consequently, when U.S. special negotiator Thomas Pinckney arrived in Spain in 1795 to discuss outstanding U.S.-Spanish grievances, he received favorable treatment and returned to America with the highly beneficial Pinckney's Treaty. In this agreement, the United States received virtually every concession that it had unsuccessfully been trying to secure from Spain for more than a decade, including a favorable settlement regarding the boundary of Florida, and the right of Americans to use the Mississippi River and deposit goods in New Orleans for reloading on ocean-going vessels.

On the downside, however, Jay's Treaty soured U.S. relations with France, even as it fueled flames of partisanship in America. Weary of the burdens of office and disgusted with the bickering of his associates, Washington in 1796 published, with Hamilton's assistance, a letter to the American people in a Philadelphia newspaper. In this so-called "Farewell Address," Washington announced his refusal to seek reelection, and urged Americans neither to divide into political parties, nor ever again to commit themselves to permanent military alliances like the one the nation signed with France in 1778.

For many years, Washington had been the glue that held together the Federalist Party, if not the entire nation. Following his "Farewell Address," cohesion within the Federalist Party vanished as Federalists scrambled to find to a new party leader.

Before the 12th Amendment [ratified in 1804] changed the process for selecting the U.S. president, the Constitution stipulated that each member selected by the states to an Electoral College be empowered to vote for two individuals for the presidency. The individual receiving the most votes, if a majority, became president, while the runner-up became vice president. The founders chose this method of selecting the president because they did not trust a popularly elected president, and they feared that if Congress had this authority, the president would become a mere puppet of the legislature.

While the Republicans wanted Jefferson to be the next president, some questioned whom the Federalists preferred. A caucus of Federalists in Congress supported Vice President John Adams to be the party's candidate in the upcoming election of 1796, with Thomas Pinckney of South Carolina their choice for the vice presidency. Not all Federalists, however, liked this slate. Hamilton, for instance, who disliked Adams, maneuvered to secure the election for Pinckney by lobbying Electoral College delegates from South Carolina to cast their second vote to anyone except Adams. When word spread about this shenanigan, Electoral College members from New England withheld their second vote from Pinckney. Thus, although the Federalist Party controlled most of the states, some Federalists who were selected to the Electoral College in 1796 voted for Adams but not Pinckney, while others voted for Pinckney but not Adams.

In the end, Adams secured the most votes in the Electoral College, but owing to the schism within the Federalist Party, the Republican Jefferson came in second place, three votes behind Adams, and seven votes ahead of Pinckney. Because Pinckney won votes in South Carolina that did not also go to Adams, had he secured all of the Federalists' votes in New England, Pinckney would have won the presidency. Instead, the Electoral College in 1796 elected a Federalist as President, and a Republican as Vice President.

Adams expressed relief with his narrow victory, stating, "I have been Daddy-Vice long enough." Jefferson also conveyed comfort in taking a back seat to Adams, telling his Republican friend Madison, "I am [Adams's] junior in life, was his junior in Congress, his junior in the diplomatic line, his junior lately in our civil government." In late December

1796, Jefferson wrote a conciliatory letter to Adams, assuring him of his "respect and affection" for his long-time colleague, and urging him to pursue peace with France, because by avoiding an unnecessary war, the "glory will be all your own." Jefferson concluded with a warning that Adams's greatest threats would not come from Republicans, but from "spies and sycophants" in his own party, a not-so-subtle reference to Hamilton and his disciples. In time, Jefferson's words would prove to be prophetic.

Without a Vice President from his own party, Adams further compounded the confusion in government when he unwisely chose to keep Washington's cabinet, most of whom were friends of Hamilton and looked to him, as opposed to Adams, for leadership. Indeed, with both the government and the people sorely divided, and with France angered by Jay's Treaty and the election of another Federalist, President Adams came into the presidency under difficult circumstances. Although the Constitution of 1787 and along with it, the Washington administration, brought economic benefits and domestic stability to the young republic, the United States throughout the 1790s still received little global respect. Even a generation after securing its independence, the United States during the Federalist Era remained a third-rate nation that could not unilaterally control its own destiny.

INHERITED PROBLEMS – FRICTION WITH FRANCE

After George Washington announced his refusal to seek reelection, Pierre Adet, the French Minister to the United States, warned that only a Jefferson victory over Adams in the upcoming presidential election would eliminate the possibility of war with France. This was not to be. In December 1796, after Adams narrowly defeated Jefferson in the Electoral College, U.S. relations with France deteriorated rapidly. According to the French Directory (the dictatorial board that now ruled France), Jay's Treaty with England violated the Alliance of 1778, and owing to this breach of contract, France no longer viewed America as a friend. When Washington sent the Federalist Charles Cotesworth Pinckney as its new ambassador to France, the Directory refused to receive him, thus essentially breaking off relations with the United States. In early March 1797, just two days before Washington left office, the Directory decreed that France would renew seizures of American ships and that Americans caught aiding the British would be treated as pirates.

Upon assuming the presidency, Adams called a special session of Congress to deal with the French crisis. Some in his party desired a war declaration against France, but Adams resisted this temptation. Acting as a moderate, Adams simultaneously asked Congress to increase defense appropriations (just in case war with France became necessary) and to approve a special diplomatic mission to France to resolve the crisis. Adams's peace commissioners consisted of Charles Cotesworth Pinckney, the diplomat France already had rebuffed; John Marshall, a Virginia Federalist who later would serve the nation for 34 years as Chief Justice of the Supreme Court; and Elbridge Gerry, a personal friend of Adams and lukewarm Federalist who later would align himself with the Republicans. The objectives of the American commissioners were to prevent war with France, to stop the confiscations of American ships, and to seek compensation for the recent French seizures of American vessels.

In October 1797, when the American peace delegation met in Paris, the French Minister of Foreign Affairs, Charles Maurice de Talleyrand-Perigord, refused to receive them. Instead, French intermediaries, later to be identified simply as X, Y and Z, delivered the message that the Americans would not be received until three conditions were met: (1) President Adams must first apologize for the unkind remarks he had made about France in his message to Congress; (2) the United States must grant France a $10 million loan to enable it to finance its conflict with Britain; and (3) the United States must pay a $250,000 bribe (the equivalent of about $2.5 million in current dollars) to Talleyrand.

Although the granting of diplomatic bribes was not uncommon in the 18th century, and the United States itself recently had offered a significant gift to the Barbary Nations to settle a dispute, the delegates in Paris had no authority to accept demands that included a bribe and a major loan. Thus, outraged at the disrespectful way that they had been treated, two of the American delegates, Pinckney and Marshall, returned home to inform the administration of the rebuff. Gerry, however, remained in France until the summer of 1778, communicating informally through third parties with Talleyrand and the Directory.

When President Adams learned of the French response to his peace offer, he allowed the secret ultimatums to be printed for public consumption. As word of the "XYZ Affair" circulated, Americans from the North to the South erupted with indignation. Newspaper headlines echoed what irate Americans shouted: "Millions for Defense But Not One Cent in Tribute."

As a result of the sudden anti-French uproar, Adams's popularity soared. Never had the bright but uncharismatic Adams been so popular among the masses. Similarly, never before had the public expressed such hostility toward Vice President Jefferson and his French-loving Republican colleagues. Across America, Federalists deprecated Jefferson and honored Adams with party toasts such as:

> The Vice-President – May his heart be purged of Gallicism in the pure fire of Federalism or be lost in the furnace...John Adams – May he like Samson slay thousands of Frenchmen with the jaw bone of Jefferson.

Accompanying the rising tide of anti-Republican sentiments was a rumor of a French plot to arm the slaves and to use them against the Anglo-Americans in the South. Whether or not the High Federalists were the instigators of the rumor, they made the most of it. Everywhere Republicans became fair game for persecution. Federalist newspapers asserted that Republican foes were ready to join the French army, and issued warnings that the immigrants, in particular the "Wild Irish," were potential threats to America's security. The blunt insinuation of these attacks was that only the Federalists could protect the homeland from French domination.

Secretary of State Timothy Pickering, a holdover from the Washington administration who privately looked to Hamilton, not Adams, as the leader of the Federalist Party, wanted a declaration of war against France. His bent for war was supported by other high-ranking Federalists loyal to Hamilton. Ultimately, these hawks did not get the war declaration, but the Congressional Federalists did secure the passing of several significant and controversial pieces of legislation.

To illustrate, in the immediate aftermath of the XYZ Affair, Congress: (1) authorized the President to deport any alien that he considered dangerous to the peace, (2) lengthened the residency requirement from 5 to 14 years for foreigners seeking citizenship, and (3) imposed fines or imprisonment for sedition on any person who published "any false, scandalous and malicious writing" that might bring the government, the president, or Congress into disrepute.

Although the Republicans in Congress defeated a stronger bill that would have made aid to France a capital offense, the Sedition Act of 1798 passed Congress in a straight party vote, and was signed into law by President Adams. The intent of this law was to silence Republican opposition to Federalist policies. To underscore this political intent, Congress stipulated that the Sedition Act would expire on March 3, 1801 – the last day of Adams's term as president.

Before the expiration of this act, courts staffed by Federalist judges indicted seventeen citizens for criticizing in print their government. The most famous of these cases was the indictment of Congressman Matthew Lyon of Vermont, a feisty Republican who once literally got into a cane-swinging/fire-tong-stabbing brawl on the floor of the House

Chamber with an equally obnoxious and ill-tempered Federalist Congressman Roger Griswold. Although Lyon's virulent opposition to Federalist policies resulted in his conviction and arrest for violating the Sedition Act, Lyon ultimately delivered the final punch in his political slugfest with the Federalists when Vermont voters reelected him to Congress even while he was serving prison time.

Lyon's continuing popularity among his constituents, notwithstanding his violation of the Sedition Act, suggested that at least in Vermont, outlawing opposition to the federal government and eliminating opposition to it were two different things. While many caught up in the anti-French war fever were willing to employ draconian measures to silence minority voices opposed to the war, the overt crackdown against opponents of the administration also convinced others that the freedoms fought for and won during the revolution were in danger of being lost.

THE BIG EVENT
FROM HAWK TO DOVE – THE SHIFTING PRIORITIES OF PRESIDENT JOHN ADAMS

In the summer of 1798, Adams joined the ranks of the anti-French zealots as he publicly promised the nation that he would "never send another minister to France without assurances that he will be received, respected, and honored as the representative of a great, free, powerful, and independent nation." Appearing in public in military dress with a sword strapped to his side, Adams told large and boisterous crowds that the survival of the republic depended on American resolve against the French menace. As the nation rallied around his call to arms, his popularity and that of the Federalist Party soared. For the first time in his career, Adams's status rivaled that of his predecessor, the venerated Washington.

Federalists in Congress followed Adams's lead with their own war mongering. Not only did Congress suspend trade with France and revoke the French alliance, but it also reacted to the crisis by creating a Navy Department, approving appropriations for the construction or refitting of 37 warships, authorizing U.S. naval retaliations against armed French ships, and inducing former president Washington to come out of retirement to lead a new, enlarged army. To pay the cost of this "Undeclared" or "Quasi-War" War, Congress enacted a hefty $2 million direct tax on dwelling houses, land, and slaves.

In the fall of 1798, Washington agreed to accept the offered command, but only on the conditions that he could select his general officers, and remain at his home at Mount Vernon until a French invasion appeared imminent. When

Adams approved these conditions, Washington selected Hamilton as his field general, thereby giving him charge of the army. In Hamilton's army, only Federalists received commissions. Although Congress never formally declared war against France, for more than a year after the XYZ Affair, the United States was engaged in military hostilities against its former ally.

Even as America was arming and taxing itself in preparation for war, President Adams was giving second thoughts to the wisdom of his belligerent stance toward France. As the months passed, several factors contributed to Adams's willingness to soften the tone of his rhetoric. Despite the popularity of his saber-rattling, the war hysteria made it difficult for him to control the Ultras in his party who saw the crisis as "a glorious opportunity to destroy [the Republican] factor." Adams signed without comment the Alien and Seditions Acts, in part because it was his nature to acquiesce to Congress on domestic matters, and in part because he agreed that strident measures were necessary to protect the security of the nation. In time, however, he became less comfortable with the wing of his party that published catchy slogans like "Traitors must be punished," "He that is not for us is against us," and "It is patriotism to write in favor of government—it is sedition to write against it."

In addition, during the second half of 1798, Adams received several intelligence reports suggesting that France was willing to enter into good faith negotiations. The first hint of this shift in French attitude came in reports from Gerry, the diplomat who although rebuffed by the French in the XYZ Affair had remained in France throughout the spring of 1798. Gerry's decision to stay in France had upset the war hawks within Adams's cabinet, particularly Secretary of State Pickering, since Gerry's presence in France made it difficult for Pickering to ask for a formal war declaration. Pickering became more furious when he learned through Gerry's correspondence that this diplomatic lone ranger was now suggesting that Talleyrand had changed his tune and was prepared to negotiate in good faith.

When the Secretary of State read Gerry's assessments, Pickering warned Adams to dismiss any promises that Gerry might give the President about the French. By early October, Gerry was back in America, meeting with Adams at his home in Quincy, Massachusetts. Just as Pickering had feared, during this visit Gerry assured the President that Talleyrand was prepared to negotiate in good faith. Adams listened to Gerry, but remained skeptical of French intentions.

Gerry's assessment, however, was corroborated during the fall of 1798 by an opinion being circulated by Dr. George Logan. Logan was a Pennsylvania Quaker who took it upon himself to travel to France in an attempt privately to negotiate a peaceful solution to the international crisis. Congress was horrified by Logan's actions, and subsequently passed specific legislation (still on the books today) that outlawed private citizens from conducting unauthorized missions to other nations. Despite this Congressional action, however, Logan's peace-mongering was having some impact on American public opinion.

Although not yet ready to reverse his policy, in his December annual address to Congress, Adams toned down his hawkish rhetoric, and even left open the possibility of future negotiations with France. While still adamant that the French must initiate the move, Adams also stated, "Harmony between us and France may be restored at her option." Naturally, the "war faction" among the Federalists was disappointed with the President's message. Pickering, in particular, expressed disgust, and after the address privately lobbied the High Federalists in Congress to declare war without the President's sanction.

By the beginning of 1799, the war fever of 1798 was no longer endemic in all quarters of the Republic. In recent months the Kentucky and Virginia state legislatures had declared the Alien and Sedition Acts to be unconstitutional, thus asserting that the states had the authority to nullify actions of the central government. These arguments, which were drafted by Thomas Jefferson (anonymously) and by James Madison, would become standard arguments used by future generations of "states-righters" who opposed federal encroachments on the liberties of individual citizens and the states. The protests from these states encouraged other Republicans to send petitions to Congress attacking the policies of the Federalists.

Large numbers of these complaints were directed against the Federalist plan to create and fund a large army. Knowing that many Americans still viewed the presence of a peacetime army as a symbol of tyranny rather than as a protector of freedoms, Federalists avoided using the term "standing army," calling it instead a "Provisional Army." This name change did little to soften the displeasure of the liberty-minded Republicans who despised not only the army but also the property tax Congress passed to pay for it.

Despite the growing protests, leaders of the Federalist Party remained determined to press on with their plans, even though by this time a French invasion no longer appeared imminent. In particular, the High Federalists wanted new legislation that would reorganize and increase the size of the old regular army to 30,000 men – three times the previous number. When the High Federalist Secretary of War James McHenry presented his ambitious plans to the President, he based his report on memoranda, ostensibly from Washington, but in fact largely drafted by Hamilton. If acted upon, the options McHenry proposed would create a permanent army that could be used not only for defense against France, but also for launching a movement into Louisiana, Florida, or even South America to acquire new lands. Other High Federalists pressed Adams to seek legislation that would empower him to declare war if negotiations with France had not begun by August 1799.

Even as Adams was being lobbied by those within his party to move forward toward war, the President received yet another report informing him of Talleyrand's change in attitude. This time the messenger was the president's son, Thomas Adams. In mid-January 1799, Thomas returned from Europe where he had been had been serving the last four years as secretary to his brother, John Quincy Adams, a U.S. emissary in Berlin. While overseas, Thomas and John Quincy had been in contact with the U.S. emissary to The Hague, William Vans Murray. Since the summer of 1798, Murray, like Gerry before him, had been receiving through third parties informal overtures by Talleyrand.

During Thomas's visit with his father, he informed the President of Murray's communications. Moreover, he also told his father that both Murray and John Quincy had changed their minds regarding the sincerity of Talleyrand, and that now both were persuaded that the French were serious in their willingness to negotiate in good faith.

Meanwhile, the High Federalists in Congress were pressing forward with their agenda. On February 6, High Federalist Theodore Sedgwick of Massachusetts told the President that the Senate was considering a reorganization bill that would give Washington the title of "General," a military rank never previously conferred. This proposal alarmed Adams. Whom did Congress intend to act as commander-in-chief: the president or the beloved ex-president? Even more troubling, Adams wondered, who would inherit such a title after Washington was gone?

In private conversations with Gerry, Adams stated that he feared that Hamilton was behind a plan to get himself an army, and with that army, he could do great mischief. In previous years, Adams had been convinced that France alone bore responsibility for the war crisis. By 1799, however, Adams was becoming more and more concerned that some within his own party were pushing the nation toward war solely as a means to promote their own personal and political agendas. As rumors circulated that Hamilton was plotting to use his army against the Spanish in Florida, and perhaps even against the Republican "radicals" in Virginia, Adams recommitted himself to the promise he delivered in his most recent State of the Union address, namely that while "we do not fear ... war, we shall give no room to infer that we abandon the desire for peace."

During the first two weeks of February, Adams received two additional critical notices. In a dispatch from The Hague, Murray sent Adams a copy of a letter from Talleyrand that stated that "whatever plenipotentiary" the United States should send to France would be "received with the respect due the representative of a free, independent, and powerful nation." Also arriving in the mail was a package from George Washington. Within this communiqué was a letter from Joel Barlow that emphatically asserted France's desire to restore relations with the United States.

This letter itself had little impact on Adams, but with it was attached a note in Washington's pen that said the General agreed with Barlow's general assessments. Washington's endorsement of a peace initiative provided Adams with a political excuse to stand against those in his party who desired war at any cost.

DECISION DAY AND ITS IMMEDIATE AFTERMATH

Acting alone, without consulting his Cabinet or any of the leaders of his party, even without informing Abigail, his wife, on Monday morning, February 18, 1799, Adams took the most decisive action of his presidency by sending a courier with a short message to the Senate Chamber. Ironically, the courier arrived shortly after the Senate had provided for the raising of an army of 30,000. He delivered the note to a stunned Vice President Thomas Jefferson, who gleefully interrupted the Senate session by reading the President's message:

> Always disposed and ready to embrace every plausible appearance of probability of preserving or restoring tranquility, I nominate William Vans Murray, our minister at The Hague, to be minister plenipotentiary of the United States to the French Republic.
>
> If the Senate shall advise and consent to his appointment, effectual care shall be taken in his instructions that he shall not go to France without direct and unequivocal assurances from the French government, signified by the Minister of Foreign Relations, that he shall be received in character, shall enjoy the privileges attached to his character by the law of nations, and that a minister of equal rank, title, and powers shall be appointed to treat with him, to discuss and conclude all controversies between the two Republics by a new treaty.

While few details are known about the moments that preceded the delivery of this note, what transpired after its reading is legendary. Of this decision Adams's biographer David McCullough writes:

> Indeed, of all the brave acts of his career – his defense of the British soldiers in the Boston Massacre trials, the signing of the Declaration of Independence, his crossing the Atlantic on the *Boston* in the winter of 1778, the high risks of his mission to Holland – one brief message sent to the United States Senate was perhaps the bravest.

Not all Federalists of Adams's day, however, described this action in such glowing terms. Senator Sedgwick, who sat stone-faced as he witnessed the reading firsthand, wrote, "Had the foulest heart and basest head in the world been permitted to select the most embarrassing and ruinous measure, perhaps it would have been precisely the one which has been adopted." Representative Harrison Otis questioned the president's sanity, while his colleague in the House Robert Harper expressed hope that on the way back to Quincy, Adams's horses might run away and break the president's neck. Pickering perhaps most succinctly summarized the sentiment of most Federalists when he declared, "every real patriot ... was thunderstruck."

Knowing that they could not dissuade Adams from nominating Murray, and that they did not have the votes to stop his confirmation, the High Federalists urged the President to allow other ministers, including Hamilton, to join Murray on the diplomatic mission. Adams agreed to the compromise, although he selected Chief Justice Oliver Ellsworth and Virginian Patrick Henry as the additions. When Henry declined, another southerner, Governor William Davie of North Carolina, secured the appointment. Adams also promised that the two new emissaries would not depart until France formally agreed to receive Murray with dignity.

Owing to the slowness of trans-Atlantic communication, and the purposeful delays engineered by Secretary of State Pickering, eight months would pass before Ellsworth and Davie would depart for France. During this time, the leaders of the war hawks, Pickering, McHenry, and Hamilton, one by one lobbied the President to reconsider the mission. In each case, Adams listened, but in the end refused to accept the arguments against an attempted diplomatic solution to the crisis. Having failed to convince the President, Hamilton personally entreated Ellsworth to refuse to sail, or at least to resign as the minister in order to delay departure. Like Adams, Ellsworth listened, but rejected Hamilton's request.

Following this final rebuff of Hamilton and his men, in early November 1799, the U.S. peace envoy left the United States for France.

After many months of negotiations, in September 1800, the American envoy signed with the French the Convention of 1800 (also known as the Treaty of Mortefontaine). By this time, Adams had fully separated himself from the High Federalists by firing Secretary of State Pickering and forcing the resignation of Secretary of War McHenry. The Convention of 1800, although not formally ratified by Congress until after Jefferson had assumed the presidency, was a product of the will and courage of John Adams.

According to the terms of the accord, the United States agreed to assume the claims of its citizens who had lost property as a result of the French seizures of American ships. At one point during the negotiations, the French had offered to pay up to $20 million for these losses. In exchange for not demanding payment for these claims, however, the United States secured from France a suspension of two undesirable treaties, the alliances of 1778 and 1786. As a result, the United States finally was freed from the "entangling alliances" that Washington argued against in his "Farewell Address."

In brief, the United States agreed to pay $20 million in alimony to get rid of an unhappy marriage. Equally important, this final act of the American war for independence ended the Undeclared War and brought about improved relations with one of the two great superpowers of the early 19th century.

POSTLUDE
LONG TERM RAMIFICATIONS – THE ASCENDANCY OF REPUBLICANISM

Terminating a war is important, but it does not always alter the course of a nation. Adams's decision in 1799 to pursue peace with France, however, fundamentally changed America in a number of significant ways.

At the time of this decision, the United States was only reluctantly a two-party state. The founding fathers that drafted the Constitution of 1787 never envisioned the division of the citizenry into rival political parties. Regional and large-state/small-state divisions were anticipated, but not division into national parties. When strong opposition to Washington's administration emerged, a two-party system evolved, much to the consternation of the beloved President who left office begrudging this development. To Washington, just as all citizens were Americans, all citizens should consider themselves to be Federalists.

Adams's ascendancy to the presidency assured Federalist control for the moment, but the narrowness of his election indicated a politically charged America. During the height of the anti-French hysteria, however, the patriotism of a party of opposition once again came to be questioned. The Alien and Sedition Acts of 1798 were not aimed at foreign enemies, but at the perceived domestic threat to the Republic – the Republican Party. Adams at first viewed the international crisis of his administration as a conflict between good and evil, and thus defended the attempts to his party to silence those who challenged the agendas of his administration. In time, however, Adams came to believe that extreme elements within his party, as well as elements in the party of opposition, threatened the ideals upon which the nation was founded.

When Adams separated himself from the war hawks, he feared this decision would split the party of Washington and allow the opposition to gain ascendancy. In 1800, his fears were realized. Adams's break with the High Federalists destroyed the political aspirations of Hamilton, but it also torpedoed his own chances for re-election.

With the party irreparably split, in 1800 Adams placed third in the electoral college, eight votes behind the Republican candidates Thomas Jefferson and Aaron Burr, who tied with 73 votes each. With no candidate winning a majority in the Electoral College, the election moved into the House of Representatives, where Burr conspired with some Federalists for support. Hamilton warded off this development, however, by urging Federalists to support his old adversary, Jefferson.

After six days of voting and 36 ballots, the House of Representative elected the Republican Jefferson as the third president of the United States. With this election, the Federalist Era gave birth to the Age of Jeffersonian Republicanism. For the first time in history, a transfer of power took place without street rioting, a military coup, a succession of states, or bloodshed. Having withstood the Election of 1800, the young Republic demonstrated that government under the Constitution of 1787, at least on this occasion, was able to withstand the strains associated with a two-party state.

EVALUATING THE REVOLUTION OF 1800

In his inaugural address, Jefferson promoted the cardinal themes of his Republican Party: state governments must be respected; the federal government must be frugal, small in size, and pay off its debts; the sacred principles of freedom of religion and freedom of the press must be honored. Jefferson also sought to reassure the Federalists by insisting that the nation must avoid "entangling alliances" and respect minority rights. "Every difference of opinion," he asserted, "is not a difference of principle…. We are all Republicans, we are all Federalists." With these words, he was not forecasting the end of party factions, but rather he was affirming that certain American ideals were above partisan disagreements.

For Jefferson, the Election of 1800 was a "revolution" worth celebrating, not simply because it peacefully brought about a change in party control, but because it reaffirmed for the world the lofty republican principles set forth in the Declaration of Independence. Two weeks after taking office, Jefferson commented about this epochal historic event, stating, "We can no longer say that there is nothing new under the sun." He was not alone in waxing about the millennial implications of his election.

During the mudslinging 1800 campaign, Federalist papers mercilessly branded Jefferson as a "howling atheist" and an "infidel," and warned Christians to hide their Bibles should he be elected, but religious leaders who supported Jefferson's commitment to separating church and state celebrated his election victory. Baptist preacher John Leland of Massachusetts captured this sentiment when he proclaimed, "Heaven above looked down, and awakened the American genius, which has arisen, like a lion, from the swelling of the Jordan, and roared like thunder in the states, 'we will be free; we will rule ourselves.'"

As president and party leader, Jefferson worked diligently to bring about political reform. Developing close ties with the leaders of Congress (in eight years, Jefferson never issued a single veto), Jefferson achieved many of his goals. Largely by reducing the size of the military by 50%, Jefferson was able to lower the cost of government and cut the national debt almost in half, even while repealing the hated direct taxes on land and whiskey. He allowed the freedom restricting pieces of legislation passed during the Undeclared War to expire without being resurrected. And whereas 99% of the federal office holders employed during the Washington and Adams administrations were Federalists, Jefferson brought an equal mix of Republicans and Federalists into the government.

OTHER BY-PRODUCTS OF PEACE – THE LOUISIANA PURCHASE

Adams's decision for peace in 1799 did more than end a war and usher in the age of Jeffersonian Republicanism. It also paved the way for the greatest real estate deal in U.S. history – the purchase of Louisiana.

In 1802, the war between France and England was halted, and Napoleon used the opportunity to dream about building an American empire. About this time, Spain informed the United States that it no longer could deposit goods in New Orleans. Without this right, the Mississippi River would be of little use to westerners who desired to sell their wares overseas. Jefferson knew that the man behind this announcement was Napoleon. Some Americans proposed taking New Orleans by force. The President, however, resisted this option, choosing instead to send James Monroe on a special diplomatic mission to France. Monroe took with him Jefferson's offer to pay France $10 million for the town of New Orleans.

By the time Monroe joined Robert Livingston, the U.S. minister to France, and presented Napoleon the U.S. offer, France again was at war with England. Needing cash, and no longer ambitious for an American empire, Napoleon made the Americans a counter offer. For $15 million, France would sell New Orleans to the United States, and throw in the remainder of the Louisiana Territory as well. 828,000 square miles of land for $15 million reduces to about three cents per acre!

Although philosophically Jefferson believed in interpreting the constitution strictly (meaning, if it does not specifically say that government can do something, then it cannot) and thus had constitutional qualms about accepting the deal, ultimately he was persuaded that it was an opportunity that could not be passed. He later justified his actions, saying:

> A strict observance of the written law is doubtless one of the highest duties of a good citizen, but it is not the highest. The laws of necessity, of self-preservation, of saving the country when in danger are of higher obligation. To lose our country by a scrupulous adherence to written laws would be to lose the law itself...thus absurdly sacrificing the end to the means.

Thus, for three cents an acre, Jefferson with his signature doubled the size of the nation, and in so doing, transformed the social and domestic history of America. By reshaping the map of the United States, Jefferson instantly altered the ethic profile of the American people, enhanced the size of the Roman Catholic minority, increased the likelihood of future interaction (and conflict) between Euro-American and Native Americans in the West and generated a great debate over the status of slavery in newly acquired territories.

This action also impacted the future of American diplomacy. When Robert Livingston, the U.S. minister to France, realized the transaction would occur, he wrote, "From this day, the United States take their place among the powers of first rank." In 1803, Livingston's statement was still more of a dream than reality. Nonetheless, he had a point. The purchase of Louisiana would forever change America's perception of itself and its place in the affairs of the world.

Who deserves credit for accomplishing this steal of a deal: Jefferson, Livingston, Monroe? Each may share some credit, but the greater contribution was made years earlier when President Adams secured peace with France and thereby placed the United States in a position to receive a serendipitous gift.

AMERICA IN SEARCH OF RESPECT – THE LIMITS OF NEUTRALITY

Notwithstanding the contributions of Adams, it was Jefferson who received the political benefits that came with the purchase of Louisiana. Unlike his Federalist predecessor, the popular Jefferson was reelected by landslide margins in 1804, and could have been reelected again in 1808 had he not refused to seek another term. Washington stepped down after two terms because he wanted to retire. Jefferson did so for philosophical reasons. A president, Jefferson believed, should not be treated like a king, and no one – not even himself – should hold this power for more than two terms. In 1808, Jefferson supported his Secretary of State James Madison who easily defeated his Federalist foe Charles Cotesworth Pinckney for the presidency.

The political reforms, economic advancements, and territorial acquisitions that transpired during the administrations of Jefferson and Madison strengthened the young republic. Stability at home, however, did not immediately translate into foreign policy successes abroad. Throughout these years, the United States continued to receive little respect in the global community of nations. Even a generation after securing its independence, the United States under the party of Jefferson and Madison remained as it was under the party of Washington and Adams: a third-rate nation without the clout unilaterally to control its own destiny.

The rivalry between the two great European superpowers, Britain and France, greatly influenced U.S. foreign affairs throughout the infancy of the young republic. Other than the brief interlude of peace in 1802, for more than two decades these two European giants engaged each other in chronic warfare. At times, this war benefited the emerging U.S. economy since nations at war often look to neutral nations to meet their wartime needs. Furthermore, as stated above, without this war the United States would not have so easily acquired the 828,000 square miles of land beyond the Mississippi River. Thus, as a result of the Franco-British wars, the United States was able to expand both economically and territorially without upsetting the balance of power among the European nation-states.

Unfortunately, however, the ongoing clash between the world's two superpowers also made it difficult for the United States, a small, developing nation, to remain at peace. Between 1793 and 1812, four American presidents—Washington, Adams, Jefferson, and Madison—proclaimed U.S. neutrality, but in the end, neither England nor France was willing to accept American neutrality as a final answer.

Moreover, during its long war with France, the British boarded merchant ships on the high seas and pressed American sailors into the British military service. For centuries, the British Crown had exercised this right to recruit sailors whenever the motherland was threatened. Distinguishing British subjects from American citizens proved difficult, so the British Navy solved the problem by embracing the simple policy: *"Once an Englishman, always an Englishman."* Notwithstanding numerous U.S. complaints and protests, during the years of the Franco-British wars, the British Navy conscripted more than 6,000 American citizens at gunpoint.

In addition, England's wartime strategy often included blockades that prevented neutral nations like the United States from trading with France. Between 1803 and 1812, the British forces confiscated more than 900 American merchant ships. France also attempted to prevent neutral vessels from trading with its enemies, but since its navy lacked the strength of the

British armada, the French managed to commandeer only about 500 American ships. Both belligerents violated American maritime rights, but the British committed the greater sin.

Meanwhile, on America's western frontier, Native Americans under the leadership of Tecumseh became agitated at the encroachment of U.S. settlers upon their lands. On November 7, 1811, the U.S. army under General William Harrison confronted these Native American warriors at Tippecanoe. Tecumseh's men fought against Harrison's army using rifles supplied to them by the British. After the Battle of Tippecanoe, growing numbers of Americans concluded that only by driving the British from Canada would they secure the frontier from further Indian violence.

By the early summer of 1812, President Madison also had concluded that war against Britain was inevitable. On June 1, 1812, Madison asked Congress for a war declaration. Although almost four in ten Congressmen and Senators opposed the war declaration, first the House of Representatives (June 4) and then the Senate (June 18) accepted Madison's request. After attempting to avoid conflict for two decades, the young nation again found itself at war against one of the strongest, if not the strongest, world power.

Americans were unprepared for war and the military's initial attempts to attack Canada were filled with missteps and disasters. Fewer Americans supported this second war with Britain and this time the British were more prepared and more determined to whip the Americans into submission. At no time in history has the United States faced a higher probability of collapse and dissolution. As the war news turned from bad to worse, the United States faced its next critical turning point.

PROBING THE SOURCES: Questioning the Justice of Outlawing Opposition

President Washington opposed the creation of a two-party state, and yet it happened under his watch. During Adams's administration, High Federalists like Hamilton favored using government coercion to silence the voices of those who threatened the homeland by undermining official U.S. policies, and Adams agreed with them sufficiently to sign the Sedition Act into law and to prosecute those indicted under it.

Below are excerpts from the act itself and from supporters and critics of it. Which of these arguments, if any, would you have found to be persuasive in the 1790s? With 20/20 hindsight, what comments can you make about these arguments today?

Document 1: Excerpts from the Sedition Act of 1798

[Document Source: *Statutes at Large of the United States of America, 1789–1873* 1 (1845), 596–97.]

Document 1 contains the Sedition Act of 1798, an act that provided the statutory authority for the prosecution of seditious libel of the President, Congress, or the government in general. This version of the act was less severe than the earlier versions considered by the Senate that would have created the crime of peacetime treason punishable by death. Section 1 of the act was used to define sedition in ways to allow the government to prosecute cases in anti-tax rebellions. Most public attention, however, focused on Section 2. The expiration date included in the act, March 3, 1801, marked the end of the presidential term of Adams's administration.

SECTION 1. *Be it enacted by the Senate and House of Representatives of the United States of America, in Congress assembled.* That if any persons shall unlawfully combine or conspire together, with intent to oppose any measure or measures of the government of the United States, which are or shall be directed by proper authority, or to impede the operation of any law of the United States, or to intimidate or prevent any person holding a place or office in or under the government of the United States, from undertaking, performing, or executing his trust or duty: and if any person or persons, with intent as aforesaid, shall counsel, advise, or attempt to procure any insurrection, riot, unlawful assembly, or combination, whether such conspiracy, threatening, counsel, advice, or attempt shall have the proposed effect or not, he or they shall be deemed guilty of a high misdemeanour, and on conviction before any court of the United States having jurisdiction thereof, shall be punished by a fine not exceeding five thousand dollars, and by imprisonment during a term of not less than six months, nor exceeding five years; and further, at the discretion of the court, may be holden to find sureties for his good behaviour, in such sum, and for such time, as the said court may direct.

SECT. 2. *And be it further enacted*, That if any person shall write, print, utter, or publish, or shall cause or procure to be written, printed, uttered, or published, or shall knowingly and willingly assist or aid in writing, printing, uttering, or publishing any false, scandalous and malicious writing or writings against the government of the United States, or either House of the Congress of the United States, or the President of the United States, with intent to defame the said government, or either House of the said Congress, or the said President, or to bring them, or either of them, into contempt or disrepute; or to excite against them, or either or any of them, the hatred of the good people of the United States, or to stir up sedition within the United States; or to excite any unlawful combinations therein, for opposing or resisting any law of the United States, or any act of the President of the United States, done in pursuance of any such law, or of the powers in him vested by the Constitution of the United States; or to resist, oppose, or defeat any such law or act; or to aid, encourage or abet any hostile designs of any foreign nation against the United States, their people or government, then such person, being thereof convicted before any court of the United States having jurisdiction thereof, shall be punished by a fine not exceeding two thousand dollars, and by imprisonment not exceeding two years.

SECT. 3. *And be it further enacted and declared,* That if any person shall be prosecuted under this act for the writing or publishing any libel aforesaid, it shall be lawful for the defendant, upon the trial of the cause, to give in evidence in his defence, the truth of the matter contained in the publication charged as a libel. And the jury who shall try the cause shall have a right to determine the law and the fact, under the direction of the court, as in other cases.

SECT. 4. *And be it further enacted,* That this act shall continue and be in force until the third day of March, one thousand eight hundred and one, and no longer: *Provided,* That the expiration of the act shall not prevent or defeat a prosecution and punishment of any offence against the law, during the time it shall be in force.

Document 2: Arguments in Favor of the Sedition Act: Remarks of Congressman John Allen, Federalist of Connecticut, July 5, 1798. [Document Source: *Annals of Congress*, 5th Congress, 2d sess., 2098.]

At the opening of debate on a motion to reject the Senate version, Congressman Allen insisted that the bill was needed to defend the new nation against the same kind of violent rebellion that had destroyed France. Convinced that Republican printers were plotting to undermine public support for the federal government, Allen insisted that it was necessary to take stringent actions to eliminate this menace. Do you agree or disagree with his arguments? Why or why not?

While this bill was under consideration in the Senate, an attempt is made to render it odious among the people. "Is there any alternative," says this printer, "between an abandonment of the Constitution and resistance?" He declares what is unconstitutional, and then invites the people to "resistance." This is an awful, horrible example of "the liberty of opinion and freedom of the press." Can gentlemen hear these things and lie quietly on their pillows? Are we to see all these acts practised against the repose of our country, and remain passive? Are we bound hand and foot that we must be witnesses of these deadly thrusts at our liberty? Are we to be the unresisting spectators of these exertions to destroy all that we hold dear? Are these approaches to revolution and Jacobinic domination, to be observed with the eye of meek submission? No, sir, they are indeed terrible; they are calculated to freeze the very blood in our veins. Such liberty of the press and of opinion is calculated to destroy all confidence between man and man; it leads to a dissolution of every bond of union; it cuts asunder every ligament that unites man to his family, man to his neighbor, man to society, and to Government. God deliver us from such liberty, the liberty of vomiting on the public floods of falsehood and hatred to everything sacred, human and divine! If any gentleman doubts the effects of such a liberty, let me direct his attention across the water; it has there made slaves of thirty millions of men.

At the commencement of the Revolution in France those loud and enthusiastic advocates for liberty and equality took special care to occupy and command all the presses in the nation; they well knew the powerful influence to be obtained on the public mind by that engine; its operations are on the poor, the ignorant, the passionate, and the vicious; over all these classes of men the freedom of the press shed its baneful effects, and they all became the tools of faction and ambition, and the virtuous, the pacific, and the rich, were their victims. The Jacobins of our country, too, sir, are determined to preserve in their hands, the same weapon; it is our business to wrest it from them.

Document 3: Arguments Opposing the Sedition Act: Excerpts from a speech of Albert Gallatin, Republican of Pennsylvania, July 10, 1798. [Document Source: Annals of Congress, 5th Congress, 2d sess., 2162, 2164.]

In his assault on the Sedition Act, Albert Gallatin rejects the assertion that individuals charged with the crime of sedition would be acquitted if their statements against the government were true. What do you think of this argument? Under what conditions, if any, would you support empowering the government to charge citizens with sedition for opposing the policies of governmental officials?

It was true that, so far as related merely to facts, a man would be acquitted by proving that what he asserted was true. But the bill was intended to punish solely writings of a political nature, libels against the Government, the President, or either branch of the Legislature; and it was well known that writings, containing animadversions on public measures, almost always contained not only facts but opinions. And how could the truth of opinions be proven by evidence? If an individual thinking, as he himself did, that the present bill was unconstitutional, and that it had been intended, not for the public good, but solely for party purposes, should avow and publish his opinion, and if the Administration thought fit to prosecute him for that supposed individual offence, would a jury, composed of the friends of that Administration, hesitate much in declaring the opinion ungrounded, or, in other words, false and scandalous, and its publication malicious? And by what kind of argument or evidence, in the present temper of parties, could the accused convince them that his opinion was true? ...

He would only observe that laws against writings of this kind had uniformly been one of the most powerful engines used by tyrants to prevent the diffusion of knowledge, to throw a veil on their folly or their crimes, to satisfy those mean passions which always denote little minds, and to perpetuate their own tyranny. The principles of the law of political libels were to be found in the prescripts of the worst Emperors of Rome, in the decisions of the Star Chamber. Princes of elevated minds, Governments actuated by pure motives, had ever despised the slanders of malice, and listened to the animadversions made on their conduct. They knew that the proper weapon to combat error was truth, and that to resort to coercion and punishments in order to suppress writings attacking their measures, was to confess that these could not be defended by any other means.

Document 4: Excerpts from the Kentucky Resolution of 1798. Jefferson created the first draft of this resolution that was passed by the Kentucky state legislature in 1798, although his authorship was not released until years later. Summarize the essence of this argument. Why do you think Jefferson did not associate his name with it in 1798?

Resolved, That it is true as a general principle, and is also expressly declared by one of the amendments to the Constitutions, that "the powers not delegated to the United States by the Constitution, our prohibited by it to the States, are reserved to the States respectively, or to the people"; and that no power over the freedom of religion, freedom of speech, or freedom of the press being delegated to the United States by the Constitution, nor prohibited by it to the States, all lawful powers respecting the same did of right remain, and were reserved to the States or the people: that thus was manifested their determination to retain to themselves the right of judging how far the licentiousness of speech and of the press may be abridged without lessening their useful freedom, and how far those abuses which cannot be separated from their use should be tolerated, rather than the use be destroyed. And thus also they guarded against all abridgment by the United States of the freedom of religious opinions and exercises, and retained to themselves the right of protecting the same, as this State, by a law passed on the general demand of its citizens, had already protected them from all human restraint or interference. And that in addition to this general principle and express declaration, another and more special provision has been made by one of the amendments to the Constitution, which expressly declares, that "Congress shall make no law respecting an establishment of religion, or prohibiting the free exercise thereof, or abridging the freedom of speech or of the press": thereby guarding in the same sentence, and under the same words, the freedom of religion, of speech, and of the press: insomuch, that whatever violated either, throws down the sanctuary which covers the others, arid that libels, falsehood, and defamation, equally with heresy and false religion, are withheld from the cognizance of federal tribunals. That, therefore, the act of Congress of the United States, passed on the 14th day of July, 1798, intituled "An Act in addition to the act intituled An Act for the punishment of certain crimes against the United States," which does abridge the freedom of the press, is not law, but is altogether void, and of no force.

WHAT OTHERS SAY: The Revolution of 1800 and Its Limits

The controversial Election of 1800 brought Thomas Jefferson to the newly built White House. Without the firing of a shot, the Federalist Party, which had been victorious in every national election since the establishment of the young republic, had been removed from power and replaced with a Republican leadership that advocated a strikingly different vision of government. In the space of one generation, the United States had doubled in population, abolished a monarchy, created two constitutions, disestablished in many states the established churches, and embraced, at least for growing numbers, an egalitarian spirit that denounced deferential politics and privileges based on social distinction. Recognizing that more still needed to be done, Jefferson called this election the Revolution of 1800, and promised to usher in a new age of reform.

For more than two centuries, historians have analyzed and debated the ramifications of this historic period in time. Presented below are excerpts from works of three distinguished modern historians who have contributed to this discussion. Documents 1 and 2 are borrowed from the works of scholars who have studied this "tumultuous" election that they argue shaped American democracy. These works include

Edward J. Larson's *A Magnificent Catastrophe: The Tumultuous Election of 1800, America's First Presidential Campaign* (Free Press, 2007), and John Ferling's *Adams vs. Jefferson: The Tumultuous Election of 1800* (Oxford University Press, 2004). The final piece is an excerpt from Rosemarie Zagarri's *Revolutionary Backlash: Women and Politics in the Early American Republic* (University of Pennsylvania Press, 2007), an insightful work that reminds us of the limitations of this so-called age of reform.

Document 1: Excerpts from Edward J. Larson, *A Magnificent Catastrophe: The Tumultuous Election of 1800, America's First Presidential Campaign* (Free Press, 2007), pp. 49, 65-66.

> Adams was now the undisputed head of the Federalist Part, despite the opposition from High Federalists within the party. Washington's death threw off the efforts of Hamilton and his allies who had been trying to persuade Washington to run in Adam's stead. With no Federalist other than Adams enjoying a national reputation, except of course the widely unpopular Hamilton, High Federalists recognized that they now had to support Adams for a second term—at least in public. Privately,

however, some continued their scheming to drop him in the end....

Federalists went into the 1800 election never having lost the presidency and firmly in control of both houses of Congress due to their strong showing in the 1798 midterm elections. With their leaders split over Adams's peace initiative with France and critical state elections going against them in Pennsylvania and Virginia, however, their prospects for 1800 had dimmed even while Washington lived. As the only person whom all Federalists admired, Washington had held the party together and given it meaning. A few years earlier, Jefferson had predicted that the nation's "republican spirit" would revive once Federalists could no longer rally around Washington. For beleaguered Federalists, their leader's passing came at a critical time. ...

Throughout the 1790s, Republicans were defined largely by their opposition to Hamilton and the High Federalists agenda. People called them "the antis." With Washington gone and their unity shattered by Adams's overture to France, Federalists were fast becoming "the antis" – defined mainly by their opposition to Jefferson and the Republican Party. The initiative heading into the 1800 election had passed from the Federalists to the Republicans by the end of January, but the outcome was far from certain and partisanship now reigned supreme.

Document 2: Excerpts from John Ferling, *Adams vs. Jefferson: The Tumultuous Election of 1800* (Oxford University Press, 2004), pp. 209, 215.

Jefferson's presidency and those of his Republican successors, Madison and Monroe, ushered in significant changes. As president, Jefferson consciously set out to banish every trace of monarchy and aristocracy that he believed had defiled Federalist rule. He eschewed a carriage and liveried servants while traveling about the capital, ... he greeted diplomats wearing casual attire. He abandoned the practice of appearing before Congress to deliver the State of the Union message.... Despite reservations about the constitutionality of the treaty in France offered to sell Louisiana to the United States, Jefferson consented to the pact [ensuring] ... that the Republic would remain a yeoman's country for generations—centuries, even—to come. ... [He] bloodlessly acquired and made accessible a vast domain, a feat that some Ultra-Federalists had dreamed of accomplishing through the use of force. What is more, the revenue generated by land sales and the tariff eliminated the necessity of direct federal taxation. Much of Jefferson's presidency was conducted in the shadow of Napoleonic warfare, but like Washington and Adams before him, he maintained the peace, giving the infant Republic more time to find its legs....

More than any other single public figure, Jefferson deserved credit for the social and political reforms that had been achieved by 1826.... [W]hen Jefferson and Adams died on that festive July 4, each was celebrated.... There was much talk of Washington, Adams and Jefferson having been the great triumvirate of the American Revolution: Washington was its sword ... Adams its tongue ... and Jefferson its pen who had written the cherished national creed ... [but] it was Jefferson who had delivered to them an America that was finally free of the shackles of the colonial era, cutting those repressive cords in the course of a presidency set in motion by the election of 1800.

Document 3: Excerpts from Rosemarie Zagarri, *Revolutionary Backlash: Women and Politics in the Early American Republic* (University of Pennsylvania Press, 2007), pp. 8-10.

From 1789 to approximately 1830, the focus of legitimate political activity shifted from a more informal and capacious politics ... to a more organized set of norms centered around voting and political parties. At the same time, the American Revolution created a new environment for women's participation in politics. Because of the nature of revolutionary politics and the rise of print culture, new opportunities arose that allowed women to participate, albeit informally, in partisan affairs and electoral politics.... [T]he spread of an ideology celebrating equality and natural rights gave women a heightened status as the possessor natural rights. A widespread popular debate ensued that explored the possibility that women, too, might one day enjoy the same political rights and privileges as men. For a few brief decades, a comprehensive transformation in women's rights, roles, and responsibilities seemed not only possible but perhaps inevitable....

Yet in the decades following the American Revolution the issue of women's rights was so explosive that ... American women and men chose to foreclose the debate rather than pursue it to its logical conclusion.... Women were excluded from government not because they lacked sufficient knowledge, intellect, or virtue but simply on the basis of their sex—because they were women. This also suggests the darker side of the democratic process: how the broadening of political opportunities for white males meant the increasing exclusion of white females.... Just as we can no longer think about the rise of American liberty during the American Revolution without also considering its underside, the role of slavery, so we should also understand that democratization for white males in the early republic resulted in the more deliberate exclusion of women from politics and governance. The consequences of this development continue to bedevil us even to the present day.

LOOKING BACKWARD/LOOKING FORWARD: Reflections on the Silent Majorities

A Placing Yourself in Time Project.

Create in your mind a fictitious character from the Federalist Era. Write a short piece of historical fiction by describing the profile and personality of this individual, and by describing how and why this character would have participated in and/or would been influenced by the Election of 1800 and its consequences. Although this is a piece of fiction, base your essay on evidence provided in this chapter.

A Project Based Learning Assignment: Reconstructing a More Inclusive Narrative

This chapter focused on the causes and consequences of a diplomatic decision made by a president. The leading characters in this story were presidents, vice presidents, cabinet members, party leaders, and diplomats, every one of whom on this occasion was an adult, white male. Gather into a group and select a demographic group or another set of characters living during the Federalist Era who were not white men. After you define a group or set of characters that you would like to investigate, reflect upon the general question "how would the individuals in this understudied group have participated in and/or been effected by the events discussed in this chapter?" You may want to subdivide this broad question into a number of smaller ones, such as: "In what ways, if any, did these players influence the events described in this chapter? What knowledge would these players have had of the events being examined? In what ways would these events have impacted their lives?"

After discussing your reflections on the broad question and its component parts, (a) create a more specific probing question about this group that you would like to investigate, (b) compose a "need-to-know" list of potential primary sources that could contain clues that would help you answer your probing question, and (c) using digital and/or library resources, assess the availability of these sources and the ease with which researchers could locate and examine them. Conclude by preparing a brief report that summarizes what insights you gained by doing these exercises. Share your conclusions with your classmates.

SUGGESTED READINGS

Ron Chernow has authored Penguin Book biographies of two men who defined this era, *Washington: A Life* (Penguin Books, 2011) and *Alexander Hamilton* (Penguin Books, 2005). Dated but still valuable treatments of the Adams's presidency include Stephen Kurtz's classic *The Presidency of John Adams: The Collapse of Federalism, 1795-1800* (University of Pennsylvania Press, 1956) and Ralph Adams Brown's *The Presidency of John Adams* (University of Kansas Press, 1975). For acclaimed biographies of Adams and his wife Abigail, see David McCullough, *John Adams* (Simon & Schuster, 2002) and Woody Holton, *Abigail Adams* (Atria Books, 2010). Award winning biographies of Thomas Jefferson include Joseph J. Ellis, *American Sphinx: The Character of Thomas Jefferson* (Vintage, 1998) and Jon Meacham, *Thomas Jefferson: The Art of Power* (Random House, 2013).

ONLINE RESOURCES

Election of 1800

Election Map

https://www.awesomestories.com/asset/view/Election-of-1800-Results

Historic Illustrations

Georgetown and The Federal City, 1801

http://lcweb2.loc.gov/service/pnp/ppmsca/15700/15714r.jpg

United States Capitol, 1801

http://commons.wikimedia.org/wiki/File:U.S._Capitol,_c._1801,_Completed_Northern_Wing_by_Thomas_Birch_(cropped).jpg

Louisiana Purchase Resources

Map

http://classroom.monticello.org/kids/gallery/image/229/Boundaries-of-the-Louisiana-Purchase/

Political Cartoons

"Congressional Pugilists" – The Roger Griswold/Matthew Lyon Brawl

http://www.loc.gov/pictures/resource/ppmsca.31832/

"The Providential Detection"

http://lcweb2.loc.gov/service/pnp/ppmsca/15700/15714r.jpg

Portraits and Paintings

Amos Doolittle's Engraving of John Adams
http://www.loc.gov/pictures/resource/ppmsca.15716/

Gilbert Stuart's Unfinished Portraits of George and Martha Washington
http://www.loc.gov/pictures/resource/thc.5a39599/

Painting of Thomas Jefferson
http://docsteach.org/documents/532932/detail?menu=closed&mode=search&sortBy=relevance&q=%22new+nation%22&commit=Go&era%5B%5D=revolution-and-the-new-nation&era%5B%5D=expansion-and-reform&page=2

Primary Sources

The Sedition Act Trials
http://www.fjc.gov/history/docs/seditionacts.pdf

Chapter 7:

Struggling for Survival, September 13, 1814: The Battle of Baltimore & the Emergence of American Nationalism

PRELUDE

On the morning of September 13, 1814, the sun rose over Fort McHenry in the Chesapeake Bay just east of the city of Baltimore. In the harbor, a young lawyer named Francis Scott Key stood on the deck of a prisoner-exchange ship anticipating the first shot of battle. British sailors scurried aboard the war ships in the harbor—the flagship HMS Tonnant, five bomb ships, one rocket vessel, and a number of frigates and sloops—each bearing aim at the defiant American fort.

At 35 years old, Key appeared baby-faced, with cherry colored hair to his shoulders and bangs to his eyes. A devout Episcopalian, he had toyed with the idea of entering the ministry, and often put pen to paper to write hymns and poems. The British had held Key for about a week while he was negotiating the release of a client who had been kept as a prisoner since the British sacking of Washington three weeks earlier. Although Key received the release of the prisoner, the British prevented him from leaving the harbor because he knew too much about the impending attack. At 7 a.m. that morning, the first British cannon shot hurled toward Fort McHenry. The flurries of cannon shot would continue for the next 25 hours.

Flying above the fort, Key saw a large American flag waving in the breeze, sometimes disappearing behind the smoke of battle, but always reappearing as if to taunt the British fleet each time the smoke cleared. Colonel George Armistead, the U.S. commander of Fort McHenry, had ordered the creation of the battle flag and Mary Young Pickersgill, a widowed seamstress and noted flag maker, had taken up the task. Along with her daughter Caroline, she created a banner thirty by forty-two feet in size with fifteen stars (each spanning twenty-four inches from point to point) and fifteen stripes (each two feet wide). Each star and stripe represented one of the fifteen states in the union. Little could she have known of the role this flag would play in inspiring a poem that would be in the memories of American children and adults for centuries to come.

As the battle of Baltimore raged into the evening with only a sliver of new moon light appearing in the night sky, in the darkness Key watched the bursts of cannon and streaming rockets pummeling the fort. Throughout the night as the battle raged, Key caught glimpses of Pickersgill's now tattered stars and stripes flying boldly over the embattled fort. So moved was Key by this experience that he penned a poem set to a popular British bar tune, "To Anacreon in Heaven."

Key's "The Star Spangled Banner" became an instant symbol of American patriotism. (In 1931, Congress declared it to be the American National Anthem.) His words preserve for all time the drama and spectacle of the battle:

> Oh, say can you see, by the dawn's early light,
> What so proudly we hailed at the twilight's last gleaming,
> Whose broad stripes and bright stars, through the perilous fight,
> O'er the ramparts we watched, were so gallantly streaming?
> And the rockets' red glare, the bombs bursting in air,
> Gave proof through the night that our flag was still there.
> O say, does that star-spangled banner yet wave
> O'er the land of the free and the home of the brave?

An overlooked verse from this song captures Key's realization of the importance of this battle to the war, to the future of the United States, and to his own wife and children who waited in Baltimore for him to return:

> O thus be it ever when freemen shall stand
> Between their loved homes and the foe's desolation!
> Bless with victory and peace, may our heav'n-rescued land
> Praise the Power that hath made and preserved us a nation.
> Then conquer we must, for our cause it is just—
> And this be our motto: "In God is our trust!"
> And the Star-spangled Banner in triumph shall wave
> O'er the land of the free and the home of the brave.

Notwithstanding Key's rhetoric, in the months that preceded the Battle of Baltimore, only a slight majority of Americans would have joined with Key in proclaiming, "Then conquer we must, for our cause it is just." In fact, as unpopular as some future U.S. wars would be, none would be distrusted by such large regions in America than the War of 1812. Why was America so divided during months that led up to the Battle of Baltimore?

THE 2ND AMERICAN REVOLUTION OR MR. MADISON'S WAR

To those who voted for the 1812 war declaration against Britain, the War of 1812 was America's second revolution against British violations of American liberties. To others, however, the war declaration was an ill-advised and dangerous gamble taken by an untrustworthy, land-grabbing political party. To these critics, it was not "America's war," but it was merely "Mr. Madison's War."

When Federalist Samuel Goodrich first learned that both the House and Senate approved President Madison's request for a war declaration, he remarked that the news "hit like a thunderbolt." He reacted this way in part because as a Federalist, he rarely supported any initiative advocated by this Republican president who was vastly unpopular in New England. But Goodrich's reaction was not simply motivated by political considerations. Like most New Englanders, Goodrich feared that Madison had drawn the young republic into a war for which it was unprepared, and which threatened to devastate the economy, and perhaps even to reduce the nation to ruins.

During the summer of 1812, alarmed citizens across New England responded to the disturbing news by closing their shops and flying their flags at half-mast. The New England discontent for war was not limited to private demonstrations. The Massachusetts House called the war decision an act of "inconceivable folly and desperation … Hostile to your interests, menacing to your liberties, and revolting to your feelings." Likewise, the Connecticut House condemned Congress for declaring war without first "counting the cost" – for charging into a war against a formidable foe "without fleets, without armies, with an impoverished treasury, with a frontier by sea and land extending many hundreds of miles, feebly defended."

Even outside of New England, enthusiasm for the war was lukewarm in many circles. Thirty-four of the thirty-six Federalist Party members in the House of Representatives circulated "An Address of the Minority" that asserted that the nation was "rushing into difficulties, with little calculation about the means, and little about the consequences." "Let us not be deceived," this stinging polemic warned. "A war of invasion may invite a retort of invasion." Within weeks after the war announcement, Federalist newspapers from New York to Alexandria to Charleston produced editorials that both denounced the war and predicted national calamity.

In some regions of the country, the war confirmed the gloomy predictions of the Federalists. For instance, in New England and in the South—areas heavily dependent on commerce and agricultural export—the wartime British blockade caused severe economic hardships to the regions. By the end of 1813, 250 idle ships sat in the Boston harbor rotting from inactivity. Shippers willing to take the risk of travel were saddled with insurance fees approaching 75% of the value of the ship and its cargo. In the agrarian South, conditions were little better. Unable to find buyers for the southern produce, commodities prices plunged so precipitously that it caused Thomas Jefferson to remark that tobacco was "not worth the pipe it is smoked in."

In other regions, particularly Republican Party strongholds, presses hailed the boldness of an administration that was willing to defend American liberties against a British regime that unapologetically kidnapped American citizens into its navy and unlawfully curtailed freedom on the seas. The *National Intelligencer* (a Republican newspaper) urged, "This is no time for debating the propriety of war. WAR IS DECLARED, and every patriot heart must unite in its support."

PAUSE-THINK-REFLECT

Do you agree or reject the general statement that after war is declared, Americans should unite in its support? To what degree, if any, does your approval of the party in power influence your willingness to embrace this general principle?

Scarcely a month after the war declaration, hostilities between the pro-war and anti-war parties turned the streets of Baltimore into the scene of an ugly riot that resulted in the destruction of Federalist printing presses and even in the death of a local Federalist leader. Although this terror in the name of national patriotism effectively silenced the anti-war voices in Baltimore, in less Republican pockets across the nation the repugnant Baltimore riots created a voter backlash that propelled the Federalist Party to wartime election victories in Maryland, New York, and New England.

In 1812, pro-war Republicans learned the hard way the same lesson that the Federalists learned in 1798 when they attempted to silence the opposition party during America's Undeclared War against France. Partisan attempts to make political gains in times of crisis by demanding national unity is a risky business that can easily boomerang on whatever majority party is in power.

1812-1814 : YEARS OF DEFEAT AND DISUNION

The anti-war voices that sounded at the outbreak of the War of 1812 were minor in comparison to the shrill expressions of opposition that were shouted two years later. Despite the early opposition of the Federalists toward the war, at least in 1812 England's problems with corralling Napoleon in Europe made the prospects for an American victory in Canada look good. At that time, even the normally politically astute Thomas Jefferson was convinced that the conquest of Canada would be "a mere matter of marching."

This optimism was not without foundation. Not counting Indians, the population of the United States in 1812 outnumbered the population of Canada 15 to 1, and in Lower Canada, where much of the war would be fought, two-thirds of the Canadians were of French origin, and thus of questionable loyalty to Great Britain.

Still, notwithstanding the population advantage, on three occasions during the early years of the war the United States invaded its neighbor to the North, and on three occasions, its forces were repelled. The failed military operations in Canada aroused concern even among prominent Republicans like Nathan Macon, who warned, "Without a change in the management of the war ... the Republican Party must go down[.] The people of every part of the Nation, will be disgusted with an administration, who have declared war, without ability to conduct it, to a favorable issue."

The offensive failures in Canada, coupled with England's conquest of Napoleon (April 6, 1814), greatly reduced the odds for a United States victory against Great Britain. The early Republican dreams of annexing Canada had vanished. In their place were more modest military objectives – defending the homeland against the world's greatest superpower, which no longer was entangled in a bitter European conflict.

With Napoleon in check, the British turned their focus and their wrath upon their "ungrateful cousins." In the summer of 1814, an additional 14,000 experienced British troops crossed the Atlantic to launch what would be a three-pronged attack against Lake Champlain, Chesapeake Bay, and New Orleans. In the middle states, an underfed, underpaid, and mostly untested American army rallied to defend the most likely invasion target – Baltimore. This strategy, however, left the capital, Washington, D.C., virtually defenseless. The British took advantage of the situation and chose to strike their first blow at American pride. On August 19, 1814, four thousand British soldiers led by Major General Robert Ross landed in Benedict, south of Washington, and marched north along the Patuxent River. The British fleet, commanded by

Struggling for Survival 221

Admiral Sir George Cockburn, followed the ground troops on the river and toward the capital.

As the British reached Bladensburg, just east of Washington, American Brigadier General William Winder destroyed his own gunboats to prevent their capture and assembled a defense force of 1,000 regular troops, 400 sailors, and 6,000 ill-trained militia. Still unsure if the British were about to assault Washington or Baltimore, Winder split his troops – half to defend Washington and half to Baltimore.

As the British rushed across the bridge at Bladensburg, most of the troops defending Washington were quickly dispersed under a barrage of rockets. President Madison, apprised of the situation, set fire to the Navy Yard and fled the city. On August 24, with the capital now virtually unprotected, the British easily marched into Washington. In a letter to her sister, Dolly Madison reported on the events of the hour:

> Our kind friend, Mr. Carroll, has come to hasten my departure, and is in a very bad humor with me because I insist on waiting until the large picture of Gen. Washington is secured, and it requires to be unscrewed from the wall. This process was found too tedious for these perilous moments; I have ordered the frame to be broken, and the

canvass taken out it is done, and the precious portrait placed in the hands of two gentlemen of New York, for safe keeping. And now, dear sister, I must leave this house, or the retreating army will make me a prisoner in it, by filling up the road I am directed to take. When I shall again write you, or where I shall be tomorrow, I cannot tell!!

According to British accounts of the invasion, the streets of Washington were filled with "soldiers and senators, men, women, children, horses, carriages, and carts loaded with household furniture, all hastening toward a wooden bridge which crosses the Potomac. The confusion thus occasioned was terrible, and the crowd upon the bridge was such as to endanger its giving way." In this night of confusion and terror, the British troops burned the Capitol, the President's house, the Treasury, the War Office, and the office of the *National Intelligencer*. A British soldier reported, "of the senate-house, the President's palace, the barracks, the dockyard, etc., nothing could be seen, except heaps of smoking ruins; and even the bridge, a noble structure upward of a mile in length, was almost wholly demolished." With this victory easily in hand, the British turned their efforts toward Baltimore – America's third most populated city.

THE BIG EVENT
TURNING OF THE TIDE – THE BATTLE OF BALTIMORE

When the British navy set up blockades of the Chesapeake harbor in response to the United States' declaration of war, the defiant citizens of Baltimore took action. Their sailors in swift schooners threaded the barriers, attacked British ships, and seized cargo in an effort to keep some flow of trade alive. Because of these actions, the British accused Baltimore of being no more than "a nest of pirates," and threatened reprisals.

In anticipation of a navy assault against Baltimore, concerned citizens scurried to shore up Fort McHenry, a large earthen entrenchment that protected the city from the east. In 1813, Fort McHenry received substantial improvements – including a 32-pound cannon, hotshot furnaces (used to create flaming projectiles), and additional batteries along the Patapsco River.

On September 12, British Major General Ross led a command of 5,000 land and sea forces up the eastern coast from Washington, through the Chesapeake Bay, up the

Patapsco River and to a place northeast of Baltimore called North Point. His ships landed at 3:00 a.m. and began transferring soldiers to shore. By 7:00 a.m., they were ready to march on Baltimore. American Brigadier John Stricker had anticipated the landing and took a brigade of 3,185 men to meet the British. A volunteer force of 250 men advanced to the British lines and in a brief skirmish the commanding British General Ross received a mortal wound. Rear Admiral George Cockburn quickly took command of the British troops and marched toward Baltimore, but was turned back at Hampstead Hill by determined American forces. There, the British army elected to wait for its navy to shell and subdue the city before resuming its attack.

  In the early morning light of September 13, 1814, the British navy began its assault, firing cannon balls, rockets, and bombs into Fort McHenry. For twenty-five hours the rumble and flash of battle continued. In all, the British fired over 1,500 rounds into Fort McHenry. Amazingly, American casualties numbered only four dead and twenty-four wounded. During the battle, when the British ships ventured closer, they were repelled by heavy fire: hotshot cannonballs. By the morning of September 14, the British realized that their attack had failed. They withdrew back to North Point and picked up their retreating soldiers.

Only two days before the Battle of Baltimore, an American convoy in Plattsburgh Bay in the northern frontier had defeated another fleet in the British navy. Early in this battle for the control of Lake Champlain, British cannons delivered broadsides into the U.S. flagship, the *Saratoga*, killing or wounding forty of its crew. Although momentarily stunned, the American sailors took heart when a rooster angered by the destruction of its coop flew into the smoke of the battle and crowed loudly. Cheering the fowl's act of defiance, the Americans resumed their battle positions and returned shot volley-for-volley. By the end of the day, the Americans had seized or destroyed four British ships carrying 75 guns, forced the British land forces to retreat back into Canada (leaving behind them great quantities of needed supplies), and gained undisputed mastery of Lake Champlain.

This rousing victory, which stunted Britain's northern offensive, followed by the military draw at Baltimore, which halted Britain's assault in the Chesapeake and redeemed the nation from the humiliation of the sacking of Washington, broke the string of military successes that the British had enjoyed during the preceding months of the war. The national crisis of 1814 was not yet over, but the tide of war had turned. After September 13, 1814, the United States had more cards in its hand to play while it attempted to negotiate a settlement that would end the second war for independence with honor.

NEGOTIATING THE TREATY OF GHENT – AMERICA'S CHRISTMAS GIFT

One of the greatest wonders in American history is that the United States—a politically divided, bankrupt, second-rate nation with a pre-war navy of 16 ships—was able to negotiate a favorable end to the War of 1812 – a war that was waged against the world's preeminent superpower with a pre-war navy of over 800 ships and with an experienced army that proved able during the war to ransack the nation's capital and to win control of significant sections of America's northern territories.

The story of the negotiations that ended the War of 1812 is almost as long as the war itself. On the very day that war was declared, President Madison had his Secretary of State James Monroe urge Augustus Foster, the British minister in Washington, D.C., to work for peace. Five days later Madison himself informed Foster that peace could be restored if the British would rescind the Orders in Council (and thereby stop seizing American ships trading with Britain's enemies) and end the barbaric custom of impressing American seamen into the British navy.

Madison also promptly sent word to Jonathan Russell, the American charge d'affaires in London, authorizing him to open negotiations for an armistice. By the time this word reached Russell, Britain already had repealed the Orders in Council. Consequently, from a U.S. point of view, just one month after the war had begun, only one issue stood in the way of peace – the end of impressments. During the ensuing negotiations, however, neither side was willing to budge, as the United States refused to tolerate Britain's historic method of military conscription, and Britain, having already repealed its Orders in Council, refused to grant the United States any further concessions.

In 1813, Russia attempted to jump start peace talks between the United States and Britain by inviting delegates from both nations to enter a new round of negotiations in St. Petersburg. Russia's desire to secure an armistice was motivated by more than simply humanitarian concerns. Before 1812, U.S. ships had supplied tropical produce to Russian ports in the Baltic Sea. Unfortunately for Russia, Britain's war against the United States abruptly halted this trade. More importantly, even as the United States was invading Canada with its 5,000 soldiers, Napoleon was invading Russia with 500,000 men. With Britain as its principal ally, Russia needed Britain to focus its military efforts where it meant the most – in a war against Napoleon, not against the United States.

Madison immediately embraced Russia's arbitration offer, and dispatched a team of peace commissioners to St.

Petersburg with instructions to seek British concessions on a broad range of issues (including the acquisition of Canada), but to insist upon only one non-negotiable item: the end of impressments. The American delegation arrived in St. Petersburg in July 1813, ready to open peace negotiations. Although the British did not want to offend their Russian allies, they also did not want to be forced into a third-party arbitration. Knowing that the war against the United States was going in their favor (and thus, that time was on their side), the British decided to pursue a diplomatic strategy of delay.

After months of waiting for the British to arrive in St. Petersburg, Madison received word that the British would not participate in Russia's mediation offer, but that they would consider direct negotiations with the United States at a neutral site. Madison accepted this offer, and negotiations for a conference to discuss peace terms proceeded. After further British delays and a last-minute change in the site of the meeting, the two peace delegations finally gathered in August 1814 in Ghent, Belgium, to deliberate.

The American delegates at Ghent (John Quincy Adams, Henry Clay, Albert Gallatin, James Bayard, and Jonathan Russell) were distinguished and exceedingly able politicians and diplomats. The British, in contrast, regarded the negotiations at Ghent to be less important to the Empire than the simultaneous diplomacy that was taking place at the

Congress of Vienna (September 1814–June 1815)—a multinational gathering of world powers that was reconstructing Europe following the end of the Napoleonic Wars. Consequently, while America's best and brightest were represented at Ghent, the British team consisted of less experienced, and generally less able diplomats who would consistently be outmaneuvered by their American counterparts. As Donald Hickey, the eminent historian of the War of 1812, has so aptly noted, "It was here – in Ghent, Belgium, rather than on the Canadian-American frontier – that the ... Americans could claim their most significant victory."

Several factors contributed to the American victory at Ghent. For starters, by the time the belated negotiations finally began, the British already had defeated the French, banished Napoleon to Elba, and launched what they expected to be a successful three-pronged attack against the strained defenses of the United States. These military advantages, however, turned into diplomatic nightmares for the British when their cocky yet inexperienced team of negotiators overplayed their hand. Delivering to the Americans what John Quincy Adams called "arrogant, overbearing, and offensive" notes, the British opened the negotiations by asserting a number of *sine qua non* (non-negotiable) demands: (1) Canada would acquire American territory in Maine and present-day Minnesota in order to ensure for the British an overland route between

Quebec and Halifax and a direct access to the Mississippi River; (2) the United States would remove all war ships and fortifications from the Great Lakes; (3) the American right to fish in Canadian waters and dry their catch on Canadian shores would not be renewed; and (4) the United States would cede its Old Northwest territories (including large portions of Ohio and Minnesota, and almost all of Indiana, Illinois, Michigan and Wisconsin) to Native American tribes, thus creating a permanent reservation for the western Indians that would function as a buffer zone between the United States and Canada.

Stunned and infuriated by these demands, the Americans rejected as outrageous these proposals that would undermine American sovereignty, impede America's ability to defend its borders, reduce the landmass of the United States by more than 250,000 square miles, and force 100,000 American citizens to abandon their homes. When Madison learned of the British terms for peace, he had them published for the world to see, an action that annoyed the British, who considered the public release of terms while the negotiation was in progress to be a scandalous act for "any civilized government." Whether scandalous or not, the consequence of this action was as Madison intended: it showed the peoples of Britain and of the world, and even more importantly the American Federalists, how unreasonable and degrading the British had become. Although presented as non-negotiable demands, the British prerequisites for peace in actuality were probing operations intended to delay the proceedings and to discover what concessions the Americans were willing to consider. Henry Clay, a notorious gambler with a penchant for card games, quickly surmised that the British were bluffing. Warning his fellow negotiators in Ghent that the British were "attempting an experiment upon us," Clay insisted that Britain's true intent was to delay the negotiations in the hope that "they will strike some signal blow during the present campaign." America, he advised, should make no concessions to the British, but instead should stand resolute and hope for more encouraging news from home.

Clay's instincts proved to be correct. Throughout September 1814, Lord Liverpool, the British prime minister, was instructing his foreign secretaries to prolong the Ghent negotiations, predicting, "If our commander [in America] does his duty, ... we shall have acquired by our arms every point on the Canadian frontier which we ought to insist on keeping." To Liverpool's surprise, however, the news he wanted to hear from America never arrived. Instead, the failures of the British at Plattsburgh and Baltimore dashed England's hopes for a swift and decisive victory, thus turning the cocky predictions of September 1814 into reflections of what might have been. "If we had either burnt Baltimore or held Plattsburgh," wrote

Britain's most outspoken negotiator at Ghent, Henry Goulburn, "I believe we should have had peace on [our] terms." But this was not to be. When the projected cost for another campaign against the United States came in at 10 million pounds (an amount that would require the renewing of the politically unpopular property tax), the British ministry concluded that it was time to reconsider its diplomacy of war and peace. In 1814 as in 1783, Britain ultimately decided that victory over the United States was not worth the cost.

The Treaty of Ghent, sometimes referred to as the Peace of Christmas Eve, was signed by the British and American envoys on December 24, 1814. The treaty ultimately mentioned none of the issues that had caused the war. In the final settlement, the British did not insist on any of its "non-negotiable" demands. Likewise, the United States did not insist that the British renounce impressments, although with the end of the war in Europe, at least for the moment, no American would have to worry about being kidnapped into the British navy.

The British also would not even insist on *uti possidetis*, a commonly accepted principle in international law that allowed a nation to keep possession of any territory that it occupied and controlled at the end of a war. Instead, the treaty included the language preferred by the Americans, *status quo ante bellum*, where each side agreed to restore the conditions that existed before the war began. All prisoners would be released, all conquered territory would be returned, and all troops would be evacuated without destroying enemy property or carrying off the spoils of war. Each nation also agreed to make peace with the Indians, to establish commissions to settle U.S.-Canadian boundary disputes, and to work to eliminate slave trade. At least the Americans in Ghent could celebrate Christmas 1814 knowing that peace was at hand.

THE BATTLE OF NEW ORLEANS – A MEANINGLESS-MEANINGFUL AMERICAN VICTORY

With no telephone or Internet immediately to communicate the news of the settlement, the war in America continued as if no armistice had been reached. In December 1814, Sir Edward Pekenham moved a British fleet carrying 7,500 veterans toward New Orleans. His intent was to secure control of the Mississippi River. To counter this initiative, U.S. General Andrew Jackson moved the 5,000 soldiers under his command to a point five miles from New Orleans. The American defensive position was on high, dry land between a swamp and the east bank of the Mississippi River.

On the morning of January 8, 1815, the British attacked through the swamp with a force of 5,300 men.

Jackson's troops, many of them expert Tennessee and Kentucky marksmen with long rifles, decimated the British regulars. In just one hour, General Pekenham, two other British generals, and more than 2,000 British regulars were killed or wounded. Meanwhile, the United States suffered only eight dead and thirteen wounded.

This great victory, fought two weeks after the Treaty of Ghent was signed, had no impact on the peace settlement, but it did provoke national celebrations and transform General Jackson into America's greatest hero since George Washington.

By late January 1815, rumors of the American victory in New Orleans had spread across the nation. Ironically, reports of this great victory arrived in Washington at about the same time that an anti-war group of New England Federalists were circulating proposals issued by the recently adjourned Hartford Convention (December 15, 1814 – January 5, 1815).

This extra-legal body, called by disgruntled Federalists and held in secret sessions, recommended a series of constitutional changes, including amendments that would prohibit embargoes beyond 60 days; require a two-thirds vote of both Houses to declare war; ban naturalized citizens from holding office; limit the president to a single-term; and prohibit the election of a president who resided from the same state as the preceding president, thus ending the Virginian domination of the presidency.

Although large numbers of New Englanders supported these measures during the earlier years of the war, by 1815, these recommendations that were drawn up in secrecy became the butt of popular ridicule. For years to come, the name "Hartford" would be associated with conspiracy, sedition, and treason.

Even as Americans were reveling in the victory at New Orleans, news from the American envoys in Ghent arrived. At 8 p.m. on February 11, 1815, a ship set anchor in New York harbor with the official word that peace with honor had been won. Immediately, express riders on horseback scurried out of New York in all directions, and celebrations erupted everywhere the news was received. In Boston, schools closed, bells rang, cannons fired, and celebrants with the word "peace" inscribed on their hats paraded throughout the city. In Washington, Madison sent the formal treaty to the Senate, where it was unanimously approved by a 35-0 vote. At 11 p.m. on February 17, 1815, when the formal ratification notice was given to the British minister in Washington, the War of 1812 officially was over.

Newspaper editorials across America screamed with enthusiastic hyperbole. "Not one inch of territory lost!" "We have stood the contest, single-handed, against the conqueror of Europe." "We have unqueened the self-stiled Queen of the Ocean…we have beaten at every opportunity, *Wellington's Veterans*!" According to these patriotic outbursts, the United States was able to accomplish what even Napoleon was unable to do, and that was to stand toe-to-toe with the strongest power on earth and come away un-scarred and unscathed.

POSTLUDE

THE LEGACY OF THE WAR OF 1812

The legacy of the War of 1812 was both immediate and lasting. Before the war, most Americans viewed peacetime armies not only as a waste of money, but also as a potential threat to the liberties of the people. By the end of the war, however, most viewed the standing army as a protector of American freedoms. Consequently, just two weeks after the conflict officially ended, Madison asked Congress to maintain a peacetime army of 20,000 soldiers – an army four times the size of the force that had invaded Canada only a few years earlier. Ultimately, Congress decided the price tag for this request was too high, but it did vote on March 3, 1815, to maintain a post-war army of 10,000 regulars. In 1816, Congress also authorized the construction of nine ships-of-the-line and 12 heavy frigates. Never again would maintaining a peacetime army be viewed as a symbol of tyranny. More importantly, never again would the United States enter a war as an unheralded underdog.

The war also forever altered the balance of power between the United States and its chief North American competitors, the Native American Indians. Without the continuation of support from European nations, after the War of 1812 the military power of the western tribes diminished rapidly in comparison with that of the United States. By 1818, the U.S. Secretary of War could report that the Native Americans "have, in a great measure, ceased to be an object of terror, and have become that of commiseration." This suppression of the Indian threat paved the way for western migration and made possible a spirit of conquest that later would be called "manifest destiny." As historian Donald Hickey has concluded: "The heady nationalism and expansionism that characterized American foreign policy throughout the nineteenth century was at least partly a result of the War of 1812."

The war also enhanced America's reputation in Europe. Never again would the Great European powers attempt to regulate American trade as they did during the decades that led up to this conflict. Moreover, never again would American citizens be subjected to impressments into the British military. In 1815, Augustus Foster, Britain's former minister to the United States, acknowledged, "the Americans have had the satisfaction of proving their courage—they have brought us to speak of them with respect." Although America did not emerge from its "second war of independence" as a major player in world events, it did achieve as a result of the war a level of respect that it never had enjoyed during its first four decades of nationhood.

POLITICS IN THE ERA OF GOOD FEELINGS

The War of 1812 also left an enduring political legacy. Although the economic and military difficulties the nation faced during the war itself vindicated many of the Federalist pre-war policies, including the need for an enlarged military and for a national bank, the lack of support that the Federalists gave to the war effort put the opposition party in difficult straits during the post-war period. The decline of the Federalist Party actually began with Jefferson's election in 1800, although this declension temporarily was halted during the dark days of the War of 1812. Aided by the unpopularity of what the Federalists rudely called "Mr. Madison's War," the old party of Washington and Adams made somewhat of a comeback in the Congressional elections of 1814, capturing 68 seats in the House of Representatives.

After the Treaty of Ghent, however, the Federalist Party once again was on the road to perdition. In the presidential election of 1816, the Virginia dynasty was continued as Republican James Monroe easily defeated Federalist Rufus King in the Electoral College, 183-34. A few weeks after his inauguration, Monroe set out on a tour of the nation. Even in New England he was greeted with adoration. The Boston *Sentinel,* the same paper that had reported Jefferson's election with disgust and distain, spoke magnanimously of Monroe as the herald of "an era of good feelings," a phrase that captured the fancy of the American public.

During the ensuing years, many former Federalists drifted into the Republican Party. By 1820, the Federalist Party was so weak that it decided not to even oppose Monroe's bid for re-election. As a result, in the election of 1820 the incumbent president received every electoral vote except one, and even this one dissenting vote was cast not so much to oppose Monroe as to retain for George Washington—the father of the nation—the honor of being the only president unanimously elected.

In the aftermath of the War of 1812, the nation under Republican leadership adopted nationalistic agendas that would have made the old Federalists blush. Before Madison left office, the Republican-dominated Congress established the second Bank of the United States (recall, it was the Federalists who created the original Bank of the United States that Republicans allowed to expire in 1811), passed a tariff three times higher than the controversial tariff advocated by Alexander Hamilton a quarter of century earlier, and passed a bonus bill, which if not vetoed by Madison, would have provided massive amounts of federal aid for the construction of highways and canals designed to enhance trade between the regions of the country.

This nationalistic binge continued under Monroe and extended even into the nation's foreign diplomacy. Under Monroe's nationalistic Secretary of State John Quincy Adams (the son of the former Federalist president who left the party of his father to become a Republican), the United States secured treaties with Britain that demilitarized the Great Lakes, renewed American fishing rights off the coasts of Newfoundland and Labrador, and provided for joint Anglo-American occupation of the Oregon territory. These treaties marked the beginning of friendlier relations between the United States and Britain. Never again would the United States fight another war against its former motherland.

Meanwhile, even as the United States moved toward rapprochement with Britain, Secretary Adams took advantage of a conflict with the Seminole Indians in the southern states to demand that Spain either control the Indians that lived in Florida—an impossibility—or else cede Florida to the United States. After the U.S. army under General Andrew Jackson chased the Seminoles into Florida, capturing Pensacola and St. Mark's in the process, the Spanish decided that it would be better to negotiate a solution to its problem with the United States rather than simply to lose Florida by military conquest.

Consequently, in 1819, the Spanish agreed to the terms of the Adams-Onis Treaty, which not only ceded Florida to the United States, but also fixed the boundary line between the Louisiana Territory and the Spanish southwest. This treaty often is called the Transcontinental Treaty because it in effect recognized the extension of the United States across the entire North American continent.

The crowning expression of U.S. nationalism under Monroe was expressed in the language of an address Monroe delivered to Congress on December 2, 1823. In this message, later dignified with name "the Monroe Doctrine," President Monroe boldly asserted that the United States will view as an "unfriendly" act any further European colonization in the Americas or any future European intervention into the affairs of the nations in the Western hemisphere. Although this message had little impact on world diplomacy in the 19th century, and in fact would be largely forgotten even by most Americans until President James K. Polk would resurrect it two decades later, the principle of "no-colonization" that is expressed in the Monroe Doctrine ultimately would emerge as the cornerstone of American foreign policy.

FROM GOOD FEELINGS TO BAD – THE REVIVAL OF POLITICAL STRIFE

The one party system that emerged during Monroe's administration would last no longer than the original one party system under Washington. For a brief moment following the Peace of Ghent, a flash of nationalistic fervor dazzled Americans and brought an unprecedented sense of political unity to the republic. The blaze of glory also temporarily cast a shadow over a number of divisive issues that lurked in the background. In time, these unresolved matters again would be brought to light. For example, when the territory of Missouri sought admission into the Union as a slave state, Congress debated the wisdom of this action that, for the first time, would have given slave-holding states a majority in the U.S. Senate. Ultimately, Congress negotiated a solution known as the Missouri Compromise. Maine, previously part of the state of Massachusetts, would be created and admitted into the

Union as a free state, while Missouri, as requested, would be admitted as a slave state. This agreement would maintain the delicate balance between free and slave states. Furthermore, in an attempt to settle in advance future dilemmas over slavery, the Missouri Compromise also declared that the section of the Louisiana Territory that was below the 36-30 latitude would be open to slavery, while the remainder of Louisiana north of that latitude would be free. This compromise that was reached in 1820 temporarily resolved the budding sectional crisis, but it did not settle the larger national debate over the compatibility of slavery with other basic American ideals.

After eight years in the White House, President Monroe, like Washington, Jefferson, and Madison, decided not to seek a third term of office. With this opening, five members from the same Republican Party competed for the presidency. The results of the election of 1824 demonstrated that sectionalism and one party rule were not opposites. One candidate, Secretary of War John Calhoun, withdrew just before the election to run for vice president. Among the other candidates, Secretary of State John Quincy Adams carried New England, but little else; Speaker of the House Henry Clay carried his home state of Kentucky, plus two adjoining states; Secretary of the Treasury William Crawford carried only Virginia and his home state of Georgia. The only candidate with some degree of national appeal was Tennessee Senator and war hero, General Andrew Jackson.

Although Jackson won a plurality of both the popular and electoral vote, no candidate received a majority of the electoral votes. Thus, the election shifted to the House of Representatives, which, according to the Constitution, had to select the president among the top three candidates in the Electoral College.

Clay, who came in fourth place, was not eligible for consideration, but as Speaker of the House, his endorsement carried significant weight. Clay embraced Adams, and with this support Adams won the presidency.

Following the election, Adams announced that Clay would become his Secretary of State. Followers of Jackson were infuriated by the outcome. To them, a "corrupt bargain" between Clay and Adams had been struck, a deal that literally stole the election from the will of the American people. The election of 1824 shattered the party truce that Monroe had established eight years earlier.

The Era of Good Feelings had ended, but in its place emerged an invigorated two party system that would take the nation into a new era that would celebrate the triumph of democratic government.

PROBING THE SOURCES: Expressions of Disunity and Unity in the Early Republic

Document 1: Amendments to the Constitution Proposed by the Hartford Convention (1814/1815)

Even while American diplomats were finalizing a peace agreement in Ghent, Belgium, twenty-six New England delegates attended a convention in Hartford, Connecticut, to discuss a New England response to the less-than-satisfactory war effort. Because the Hartford meetings were held in secret, knowledge of what took place in these meetings is sketchy, but some evidence suggests that at least some delegates considered secession from the Union as an option. In the end, the Convention report asserted New England's right and duty to affirm its authority over unconstitutional infringements, an argument with affinity to the principles stated by Jefferson and Madison in the Kentucky and Virginia Resolutions that were composed in 1798 in reaction to the passage of the Alien and Sedition Acts. By the time this report was released, news of Jackson's victory in New Orleans and the signing of the popular Treaty of Ghent made the Hartford recommendations appear ludicrous, if not treasonous.

Therefore resolved.– That it be and hereby

is recommended to the Legislatures of the several States represented in this Convention to adopt all such measures as may be necessary effectually to protect the citizens of said States from the operation and effects of all acts which have been or may be passed by the Congress of the United States, which shall contain provisions, subjecting the militia or other citizens to forcible drafts, conscriptions, or impressments, not authorized by the Constitution of the United States

Resolved.–That it be and hereby is recommended to the said Legislatures, to authorize an immediate and earnest application to be made to the Government of the United States, requesting their consent to some arrangement, whereby the said States may, separately or in concert, be empowered to assume upon themselves the defense of their territory against the enemy, and a reasonable portion of the taxes, collected within said States, may be paid into the respective treasuries thereof, and appropriated to the payment of the balance due said States, and to the future defense of the same. The amount so paid into the said treasuries to be credited, and the disbursements made as aforesaid to be charged to the United States.

Resolved.– That it be, and it hereby is, recommended to the Legislatures of the aforesaid States, to pass laws (where it has not already been done) authorizing the Governors or Commanders-in-Chief of their militia to make detachments from the same, or to form voluntary corps, as shall be most convenient and conformable to their Constitutions, and to cause the same to be well armed equipped and disciplined, and held in readiness for service; and upon the request of the Governor of either of the other States, to employ the whole of such detachment or corps, as well as the regular forces of the State, or such part thereof as may be required and can be spared consistently with the safety of the State, in assisting the State, making such request to repel any invasion thereof which shall be made or attempted by the public enemy.

Resolved.– That the following amendments of the Constitution of the United States, be recommended to the States as aforesaid, to be proposed by them for adoption by the State Legislatures, and, in such cases as may be deemed expedient, by a Convention chosen by the people of each State.

And it is further recommended, that the said States shall persevere in their efforts to obtain such amendments, until the same shall be effected.

First.– Representatives and direct taxes shall be apportioned among the several States which may be included within this union, according to their respective numbers of free persons, including those bound to serve for a term of years, and excluding Indians not taxed, and all other persons.

Second.– No new State shall be admitted into the union by Congress in virtue of the power granted by the Constitution, without the concurrence of two-thirds of both Houses.

Third.– Congress shall not have power to lay any embargo on the ships or vessels of the citizens of the United States, in the ports or harbors thereof, for more than sixty days.

Fourth.– Congress shall not have power, without the concurrence of two-thirds of both

Houses, to interdict the commercial intercourse between the United States and any foreign nation or the dependencies thereof.

Forth.– Congress shall not make or declare war, or authorize acts of hostility against any foreign nation, without the concurrence of two-thirds of both Houses, except such acts of hostility be in defense of the territories of the United States when actually invaded.

Sixth.– No person who shall hereafter be naturalized, shall be eligible as a member of the Senate or House of Representatives of the United States, nor capable of holding any civil office under the authority of the United States.

Seventh.– The same person shall not be elected President of the United States a second time; nor shall the President be elected from the same State two terms in succession.

Resolved.– That if the application of these States to the government of the United States, recommended in a foregoing Resolution, should be unsuccessful, and peace should not be concluded and the defense of these States should be neglected, as it has been since the commencement of the war, it will in the opinion of this Convention be expedient for the Legislatures of the several States to appoint Delegates to another Convention, to meet at Boston, in the State of Massachusetts, on the third Thursday of June next with such powers and instructions as the exigency of a crisis so momentous may require.

Document 2: Excerpts from the Missouri Compromise (1820).

In 1819, at the time when the Missouri Territory applied for admission as a state, the United States included 22 states, 11 of which allowed and 11 of which prohibited slavery. If Missouri were allowed entrance as a slave state, for the first time a majority of the states in the Union would be slave states. Following a stormy debate in Congress over the admission of Missouri, a compromise eventually was reached that admitted Missouri as a slave state and created a new state of Maine (formerly part of Massachusetts) that would enter the Union as a free state, thus maintaining an even balance of free and slave states. The compromise package also explicitly prohibited slavery in Louisiana Purchase lands north of the 36 degree, 30 minutes north latitude. Below are excerpts from the bill that authorized Missouri's admission. What attitudes about the appropriate form and duties of government are suggested in the language of this piece of legislation?

> *An Act to authorize the people of the Missouri territory to form a constitution and state government, and for the admission of such state into the Union on an equal footing with the original states, and to prohibit slavery in certain territories.*
>
> Be it enacted by the Senate and House of Representatives of the United States of America, in Congress assembled, That the inhabitants of that portion of the Missouri territory included within the boundaries herein after designated, be, and they are hereby, authorized to form for themselves a constitution and state government, and to assume such name as they shall deem proper; and the said state, when formed, shall be admitted into the Union, upon an equal footing with the original states, in all respects whatsoever.
>
> SEC. 2. And be it further enacted, That the said

state shall consist of all the territory included within the following boundaries.... [after the boundaries are defined, the bill continues] Provided, The said state shall ratify the boundaries aforesaid. And provided also, That the said state shall have concurrent jurisdiction on the river Mississippi, and every other river bordering on the said state so far as the said rivers shall form a common boundary to the said state; and any other state or states, now or hereafter to be formed and bounded by the same, such rivers to be common to both; and that the river Mississippi, and the navigable rivers and waters leading into the same, shall be common highways, and for ever free, as well to the inhabitants of the said state as to other citizens of the United States, without any tax, duty impost, or toll, therefore, imposed by the said state.

SEC. 3. And be it further enacted, That all free white male citizens of the United States, who shall have arrived at the age of twenty-one years, and have resided in said territory: three months previous to the day of election, and all other persons qualified to vote for representatives to the general assembly of the said territory, shall be qualified to be elected and they are hereby qualified and authorized to vote, and choose representatives to form a convention, who shall be apportioned amongst the several counties as follows....

SEC. 4. And be it further enacted, That the members of the convention thus duly elected, shall be, and they are hereby authorized to meet at the seat of government of said territory on the second Monday of the month of June next; and the said convention, when so assembled, shall have power and authority to adjourn to any other place in the said territory, which to them shall seem best for the convenient transaction of their business; and which convention, when so met, shall first determine by a majority of the whole number elected, whether it be, or be not, expedient at that time to form a constitution and state government for the people within the said territory, as included within the boundaries above designated; and if it be deemed expedient, the convention shall be, and hereby is, authorized to form a constitution and state government; or, if it be deemed more expedient, the said convention shall provide by ordinance for electing representatives to form a constitution or frame of government; which said representatives shall be chosen in such manner, and in such proportion as they shall designate; and shall meet at such time and place as shall be prescribed by the said ordinance; and shall then form for the people of said territory, within the boundaries aforesaid, a constitution and state government: Provided, That the same, whenever formed, shall be republican, and not repugnant to the constitution of the United States; and that the legislature of said state shall never interfere with the primary disposal of the soil by the United States, nor with any regulations Congress may find necessary for securing the title in such soil to the bona fide purchasers; and that no tax shall be imposed on lands the property of the United States; and in no case shall non-resident proprietors be taxed higher than residents.

SEC. 5. And be it further enacted, That until the next general census shall be taken, the said state shall be entitled to one representative in the House of Representatives of the United States.

SEC. 6. And be it further enacted, That the following propositions be, and the same are hereby, offered to the convention of the said territory of Missouri, when formed, for their free acceptance or rejection, which, if accepted by the convention, shall be obligatory upon the United States: First. That section numbered sixteen in every township, and when such section has been sold, or otherwise disposed of, other lands equivalent thereto, and as contiguous as may be, shall be granted to the state for the use of the inhabitants of such township, for the use of schools. Second. That all salt springs, not exceeding twelve in number, with six sections of land adjoining to each, shall be granted to the said state for the use of said state, the same to be selected by the legislature of the said state, on or before the first day of January, in the year one thousand eight hundred and twenty-five; and the same, when so selected, to be used under such terms, conditions, and regulations, as the legislature of said state shall direct: Provided, That no salt spring, the right whereof now is, or hereafter shall be, confirmed or adjudged to any individual or individuals, shall, by this section, be granted to the said state: And provided also, That the legislature shall never sell or lease the same, at anyone time, for a longer period than ten years, without the consent of Congress. Third. That five per cent. of the net proceeds of the sale of lands lying within the said territory or state, and which shall be sold by Congress, from and after the first day of January next, after deducting all expenses incident to the same, shall be reserved for making public roads and canals, of which three fifths shall be applied to those objects within the state, under the direction of the legislature thereof; and the other two fifths in defraying, under the direction of Congress, the expenses to be incurred in making of a road or roads, canal or canals, leading to the said state. Fourth. That four entire sections of land be, and the same are hereby, granted to the said state, for the purpose of fixing their seat of government thereon; which said sections shall, under the direction of the legislature of said state, be located, as near as may be, in one body, at any time, in such townships and ranges as the legislature aforesaid may select, on any of the public lands of the United States: Provided, That such locations shall be made prior to the public sale of the lands of the United States surrounding such location. Fifth. That thirty-six sections, or one entire township, which shall be designated by the President of the United States, together with the other lands heretofore reserved for that purpose, shall be reserved for the use of a seminary of learning, and vested in the legislature of said state, to be appropriated solely to the use of such seminary by the said legislature: Provided, That the five foregoing propositions herein offered, are on the condition that the convention of the said state shall provide, by an ordinance, irrevocable without the consent or the United States, that every and each tract of land sold by the United States, from and after the first day of January next, shall remain exempt from any tax laid by order or under the authority of the state, whether for state, county, or township, or any other purpose whatever, for the term of five years from and after the day of sale; And further, That the bounty lands granted, or hereafter to be granted, for military services during the late war, shall, while they continue to be held by the patentees, or their heirs remain exempt as aforesaid from taxation for the term of three year; from and after the date of the patents respectively.

SEC. 7. And be it further enacted, That in case a constitution and state government shall be formed for the people of the said territory of Missouri, the said convention or representatives, as soon thereafter as may be, shall cause a true and attested copy of such constitution or frame of state government, as shall be formed or provided, to be transmitted to Congress.

SEC. 8. And be it further enacted. That in all that territory ceded by France to the United

States, under the name of Louisiana, which lies north of thirty-six degrees and thirty minutes north latitude, not included within the limits of the state, contemplated by this act, slavery and involuntary servitude, otherwise than in the punishment of crimes, whereof the parties shall have been duly convicted, shall be, and is hereby, forever prohibited: Provided always, That any person escaping into the same, from whom labour or service is lawfully claimed, in any state or territory of the United States, such fugitive may be lawfully reclaimed and conveyed to the person claiming his or her labour or service as aforesaid.

APPROVED, March 6, 1820.

Document 3: Excerpts from the Monroe Doctrine (1823).

In 1823, when Britain invited the United States to denounce with her the circulating reports of French and Spanish plans to re-establish colonies in Latin America, Secretary of State John Quincy Adams advised President Monroe against signing any bilateral agreement that could limit U.S. colonial ambitions into the Americas. Thus, rather than joining Britain with a bilateral condemnation of future colonization in the Americas, Adams encouraged Monroe to boldly and unilaterally forewarn European powers against interfering into Western Hemisphere affairs. In response to this advice, President Monroe articulated such a policy in his December 1823 annual address to Congress. Although at the time, European powers feared Britain's powerful navy far more than Monroe's tough talking, in the 20th century this policy, known as Monroe's Doctrine, would play a major role in world events. In the early national period, however, Monroe's declaration was more symbolic than substantial, although it did express America's determination to be treated with respect among the major global powers. Printed below are excerpts from Monroe's address.

> At the proposal of the Russian Imperial Government, made through the minister of the Emperor residing here, a full power and instructions have been transmitted to the minister of the United States at St. Petersburg to arrange by amicable negotiation the respective rights and interests of the two nations on the northwest coast of this continent. A similar proposal has been made by His Imperial Majesty to the Government of Great Britain, which has likewise been acceded to.

The Government of the United States has been desirous by this friendly proceeding of manifesting the great value which they have invariably attached to the friendship of the Emperor and their solicitude to cultivate the best understanding with his Government. In the discussions to which this interest has given rise and in the arrangements by which they may terminate the occasion has been judged proper for asserting, as a principle in which the rights and interests of the United States are involved, that the American continents, by the free and independent condition which they have assumed and maintain, are henceforth not to be considered as subjects for future colonization by any European powers...

It was stated at the commencement of the last session that a great effort was then making in Spain and Portugal to improve the condition of the people of those countries, and that it appeared to be conducted with extraordinary moderation. It need scarcely be remarked that the results have been so far very different from what was then anticipated. Of events in that quarter of the globe, with which we have so much intercourse and from which we derive our origin, we have always been anxious and interested spectators. The citizens of the United States cherish sentiments the most friendly in favor of the liberty and happiness of their fellow-men on that side of the Atlantic. In the wars of the European powers in matters relating to themselves we have never taken any part, nor does it comport with our policy to do so. It is only when our rights are invaded or seriously menaced that we resent injuries or make preparation for our defense. With the movements in this hemisphere we are of necessity more immediately connected, and by causes which must be obvious to all enlightened and impartial observers. The political system of the allied powers is essentially different in this respect from that of America. This difference proceeds from that which exists in their respective Governments; and to the defense of our own, which has been achieved by the loss of so much blood and treasure, and matured by the wisdom of their most enlightened citizens, and under which we have enjoyed unexampled felicity, this whole nation is devoted. We owe it, therefore, to candor and to the amicable relations existing between the United States and those powers to declare that we should consider any attempt on their part to extend their system to any portion of this hemisphere as dangerous to our peace and safety. With the existing colonies or dependencies of any European power we have not interfered and shall not interfere. But with the Governments who have declared their independence and maintain it, and whose independence we have, on great consideration and on just principles, acknowledged, we could not view any interposition for the purpose of oppressing them, or controlling in any other manner their destiny, by any European power in any other light than as the manifestation of an unfriendly disposition toward the United States. In the war between those new Governments and Spain we declared our neutrality at the time of their recognition, and to this we have adhered, and shall continue to adhere, provided no change shall occur which, in the judgement of the competent authorities of this Government, shall make a corresponding change on the part of the United States indispensable to their security.

The late events in Spain and Portugal shew that Europe is still unsettled. Of this important fact no stronger proof can be adduced than that the allied powers should have thought it proper, on any principle satisfactory to themselves, to have interposed by force in the internal concerns of Spain. To what extent such interposition may be carried, on the same principle, is a question in which all independent powers whose governments differ from theirs are interested, even those most remote, and surely none of them more so than the United States. Our policy in regard to Europe, which was adopted at an early stage of the wars which have so long agitated that quarter of the globe, nevertheless remains the same, which is, not to interfere in the internal concerns of any of its powers; to consider the government de facto as the legitimate government for us; to cultivate friendly relations with it, and to preserve those relations by a frank, firm, and manly policy, meeting in all instances the just claims of every power, submitting to injuries from none. But in regard to those continents circumstances are eminently and conspicuously different.

It is impossible that the allied powers should extend their political system to any portion of either continent without endangering our peace and happiness; nor can anyone believe that our southern brethren, if left to themselves, would adopt it of their own accord. It is equally impossible, therefore, that we should behold such interposition in any form with indifference. If we look to the comparative strength and resources of Spain and those new Governments, and their distance from each other, it must be obvious that she can never subdue them. It is still the true policy of the United States to leave the parties to themselves, in hope that other powers will pursue the same course....

WHAT OTHERS SAY: Making Sense of the War of 1812

Can a war that ends by embracing the status quo that existed before the war began be consequential? To three distinguished historians of the war—Donald Hickey, Alan

Taylor, and Gene Allen Smith—the answer is a resounding yes, even if they offer different assessments of the legacy of the conflict.

Document 1: Excerpts from Donald R. Hickey, *The War of 1812: A Forgotten Conflict* (University of Illinois Press, 1989), pp. 300, 308-309.

> The War of 1812 is often called America's "second war of independence." The issues and ideology of this conflict echoed those of the Revolution.... Nonetheless, the supposed threat to American independence in 1812 was more imagined than real. It existed mainly in the minds of thin-skinned Republicans ... unable to shake the ideological legacy of the Revolution and interpreted all British actions accordingly.
>
> British encroachment on American rights were certainly both real and serious. But throughout this period the focus of British policy was always on Europe. The overriding objective of the British government was to secure the defeat of France.... Her aim was not to subvert American independence but to win

the war in Europe. Once this objective was achieved, her infringements on American rights would cease.

Not only did Republicans misread British intentions, but throughout this turbulent era they consistently overrated America's ability to win concessions...

Federalists protested that they were made scapegoats for the failure of Republican policies.... These protests fell on deaf ears.... It mattered not that the war had vindicated so many Federalist policies—particularly the importance of military and naval preparedness and the need for internal taxes and a national bank... It mattered not that Federalists had predicted the futility of the conflict and that the Treaty of Ghent had proven them right. What mattered was that the nation had emerged from the war without surrendering any rights or territory and with just enough triumphs—both on land and on sea—to give the appearance of victory.... Thus the War of 1812 passed into history not as a futile and costly struggle in which the United States had barely escaped dismemberment ... but as a glorious triumph in which the nation had single-handedly defeated the conqueror of Napoleon and the Mistress of the Seas.

Document 2: Excerpts from Alan Taylor, *The Civil War of 1812: American Citizens, British Subjects, Irish Rebels and Indian Allies* (Alford A. Knopf, 2010), pp. 10,12, 458.

The War of 1812 looms small in American memory, forgotten as insignificant because it apparently ended as a draw that changed no boundary and no policy. At best, Americans barely recall the war for a handful of patriotic episodes: for the resistance of Fort McHenry to British bombardment, which inspired the national anthem; … for the British perfidy in burning the White House and the Capitol; for the payback taken by Andrew Jackson's Tennessee riflemen at the Battle of New Orleans. These images suggest a defensive triumph against British aggression which obscures the war's origins and primacy as an American invasion of Canada. Of course, Canadians primarily remember what

Americans forget, celebrating their victory as David over the American Goliath...

Both Republicans and Loyalists suspected that the continent was not big enough for their rival systems: republic and mixed constitution. One or the other would have to prevail in the house divided. Like the revolution, the War of 1812 was a civil war between competing visions of America: one still loyal to the empire and the other defined by its republican revolution against that empire. But neither side would reap what it expected from the war. Frustrated in their fantasies of smashing the other, the Loyalists and the Republican Americans had to learn how to share the continent and to call coexistence victory....

By producing a military stalemate, the war led to a sharper distinction between Upper Canada and the United States. The destruction wrought by the invaders alienated most of the American colonists from their brethren in the republic and the postwar surge in Scotts and Irish immigrants generated the colony's new majority. In postwar Upper Canada, the people and their culture became more committed to the mixed constitution and to the union of the empire.

Document 3: Excerpts from Gene Allen Smith, *The Slaves' Gamble: Choosing Sides in the War of 1812* (Palgrave Macmillan, 2013), pp. 214-216.

[T]he monarchial British made large-scale use of slaves as soldiers, and the American republic relied on free white men instead. Using slaves as soldiers came to represent a dichotomy that did not bode well for blacks in the United States, and they would not be permitted to participate on such a big stage again until the American Civil War.

The results of the War of 1812 were undeniable for slavery. The opening of lands in the Old Southwest brought three new cotton areas into production: Natchez, Mississippi, and Baton Rouge, Louisiana… These three regions had witnessed racial unrest during the War of 1812, and American leaders had cautiously negotiated with Indians and blacks, promising favorable conditions for their assistance. Once the British war ended, whites removed the Indians from the area and then relegated free blacks and slaves to subservient positions. By 1819, Alabama had joined Mississippi (1817) and Louisiana (1812) as slaveholding states, and cotton soon became the staple that ensured the region's economic success... Before the war, slavery had also been concentrated in the Atlantic states.... By defeating the British and the Indians in the South and emasculating the Spanish in Florida, Americans spread their reinvigorated slave system southward and westward across the Gulf, giving them access to these new fertile lands for cotton cultivation.... In the end, the free blacks and slaves who Andrew Jackson had mobilized and called "Sons of Freedom," like those who had joined with the British, wanted only one thing – their land of the *free*. The War of 1812 provided the last opportunity for blacks as a group to secure that freedom through force of arms until the American Civil War finally ended slavery once and for all.

LOOKING BACKWARD/LOOKING FORWARD: Constructing a National Narrative

Reflecting on Democracy in the Early Republic:

In the Election of 1820, all members of the Electoral College except one voted for the reelection of President Monroe. After reviewing the material presented in this volume and, if you like, exploring additional secondary and primary sources, write a 500-word essay in which you address the following question: Is it appropriate to conclude from the result of the Electoral College voting in 1820 that the majority of the inhabitants living in U.S. territory at this time supported Monroe's reelection? Why or why not? Justify your answer with primary source evidence.

A Project-Base-Learning Project: Constructing a History of the Early Republic

The central theme and subtitle of *10 Days That Changed America, Volume 2* is "Building a Nation." Divide into a group and review the period between the Treaty of 1763 that ended the Seven Years' War and President Monroe's address to Congress in 1823 in which he announced what is known as the Monroe Doctrine. Assume that you were asked to create a three-chapter history that tells the story of the formation of the United States of America during this era. Create an annotated Table of Contents for this volume. Include with this outline a brief justification for the content you would include in each of the three chapters. You may construct your narrative in any way that does not duplicate the organization presented in this textbook. Convert your Annotated Table of Contents into a PowerPoint presentation and share your book prospectus with your classmates.

SUGGESTED READINGS

For an excellent overview of the war from a transatlantic prospective, see J.C.A. Stagg, *The War of 1812: Conflict for a Continent* (Cambridge University Press, 2012). Hugh Howard's *Mr. and Mrs. Madison's War: America's First Couple and the Second War for Independence* (Bloomsbury Press, 2012) is an interesting overview from an American point of view. For a more focused account of the central event discussed in this chapter, see Charles G. Muller, *The Darkest Day: The Washington-Baltimore Campaign During the War of 1812* (University of Pennsylvania Press, 1963). Students interested in the naval aspects of the war will want to read George C. Daughan, *1812: The Navy's War* (Basic Books, 2011). An excellent interpretation on the causes of the conflict is Paul A. Gilje, *Free Trade and Sailors' Rights in the War of 1812* (Cambridge University Press, 2013). For a collection of interpretations on the legacy of the war, see Pietro S. Nivola and Peter J. Kastor, editors, *What So Proudly We Hailed: Essays on the Contemporary Meaning of the War of 1812* (Brookings Institution Press, 2012).

ONLINE RESOURCES

Historical Illustrations and Paintings

A View of the Bombardment of Fort McHenry
http://en.wikipedia.org/wiki/Battle_of_Baltimore#mediaviewer/File:Ft._Henry_bombardement_1814.jpg

The Burning of Washington
http://en.wikipedia.org/wiki/Burning_of_Washington#mediaviewer/File:BurningofWashington1814.jpg

George Munger's "The President's House"
http://en.wikipedia.org/wiki/Burning_of_Washington#mediaviewer/File:The_President%27s_House_by_George_Munger,_1814-1815_-_Crop.jpg

Luke Clennell's "The Press-Gang"
http://en.wikipedia.org/wiki/War_of_1812#mediaviewer/File:Luke_Clennell02.jpg

Maps

Battle of Baltimore
http://robertluisrabello.com/just-war/battle_of_baltimore/#gallery[default]/0/

Battles of the War of 1812
http://www.maps.com/ref_map.aspx?pid=11315

Missouri Compromise
http://www.pbs.org/wgbh/americanexperience/features/general-article/lincolns-political-landscape/

Political Cartoons

John Bull and the Baltimoreans
http://en.wikipedia.org/wiki/Battle_of_Baltimore#mediaviewer/File:WilliamCharlesJohnBullAndTheBaltimoreans.jpg

Streaming Political Cartoons of the War of 1812
http://www.navy.mil/1812/gallery/photoGallery.asp?id=9

Videos

The Battle of Baltimore
http://www.1812battles.com/home.html

The War of 1812 PBS Documentary (1 hour, 53 minute film)
http://www.pbs.org/wgbh/americanexperience/features/general-article/lincolns-political-landscape/

INDEX

12th Amendment 155
Abraham (Abram) 42-43
Adam and Eve 17, 63
Adams-Onis Treaty 241
Adams, Abigail 171, 208
Adams, John Quincy 169, 228-229, 240-244, 259-260
Adams, John 37, 57, 73, 77, 80, 89, 141-144, 159-177, 180, 183-188, 200-203, 208, 210, 239
Adams, Thomas 169
Adet, Pierre 158
Africans 60, 125
Alien Act 167, 177
Allen, John 191-194
Alliance of 1778 84, 152, 158
Althusius, Johannes 59
American Dream 55, 82
American Revolution 57-58, 69, 84, 89, 151, 203-205
Amherst, Jeffrey 65
An Address of the Minority 216
Anglicans 61
Appalachian Mountains 66
Aristotle 58
Armed Neutrality 84
Armistead, George 212
Armitage, David 133, 137
Arnold, John H 50
Articles of Confederation 80, 85, 88, 91, 92
Atlantic Ocean 65, 173, 174, 220
Attucks, Crispus 69
Augustine, Saint 59

authenticity of sources 26
Baltic Sea 227
Baltimore 211-215, 218, 220-221, 223-225, 231, 273-274
Barbary Nations 160
Barlow, Joel 171
Baton Rouge, Louisiana 270
Battle of Baltimore 211-215, 223-225, 273-274
Battle of New Orleans 233-235, 245, 268
Battle of Tippecanoe 186
Bayard, James 228
Becker, Carl 136
Berlin 169
Beze, Theodore 59
Bible 17, 18, 19, 21, 41, 43
Bill of Rights 91, 144, 149
Bladensburg 221
Bloch, Marc 49
Boston 61, 69, 70, 74, 173, 217, 235, 239, 250
Boston Massacre 70, 74, 173
Boston Tea Party 70
Boyd, Julian 136
Britain 37, 64, 66-68, 74-77, 83, 84, 89, 95, 96, 99, 105, 107, 109, 132, 150-154, 159, 184, 186, 187, 215, 219, 220, 225-227, 230-232, 238, 240, 241, 259, 260
British Crown 64, 65, 66, 72, 74, 76, 83, 109, 185
British West Indies 153
Brown, Ralph Adams 208
Burn, A.F. 44
Burr, Aaron 177
Calhoun, John 243
Calvin, John 59

Canada 83, 84, 186, 219, 220, 225-230, 236, 268, 269
Carlyle, Thomas 47, 112
Carr, E.H. 49
Carroll, Charles 82, 221
Catherine the Great 83
Chernow, Ron 208
Chesapeake Bay 211, 220, 223
Christians 58, 179
Clay, Henry 228, 231, 243, 244
Clennell, Luke 274
Clio 34
Clymer, George 89
Cockburn, George 221, 224
Coercive Acts 70, 71
Columbus, Christopher 37
Committee of Five 73
Common Sense 72, 93-96
Comte, August 48
Concord, Massachusetts 71
Congress of Vienna 229
Connecticut 112, 191, 216, 245
Constitution of 1787 88, 89, 90, 91, 92, 93, 110-124
Continental Congress (2nd) 71-82
Continental Congress (1st) 71
Crawford, William 243
Daughan, George 273
David, King 91
Declaration of Independence 56, 79-82, 85, 89, 91, 97-110, 125, 128, 131-137
Declaration of Rights and Sentiments 79, 125, 126-127
Declaratory Act 69

Delaware 77, 112
Democratic Party 148
Democratic Republican 148
Denmark 84
Dickinson, John 77
direct taxes 68, 111, 122, 164, 180, 203
Doolittle, Amos 210
Douglas, Frederick 125, 128-130
Dover, Delaware 76
Dunlan, John 138
Dyer, Justin Buckley 137
East India Tea Company 70
Election of 1796 155, 157
Election of 1800 178, 179, 199, 200, 202, 204, 206, 208
Election of 1816 239
Election of 1820 239, 272
Election of 1824 243, 244
Electoral College 155, 156, 158, 177, 239, 244, 272
Ellis, Joseph J. 208
English 60-67, 72, 103, 134, 185
Era of Good Feelings 238-242
European 63, 134, 184, 220, 237, 241, 260-263
Farewell Address 154, 155, 175
Federalist Era 143, 157, 178, 206, 207
Federalists 91, 92, 145, 148, 149, 155, 156, 161-170, 173-180, 187, 200-203, 217-219, 230, 234, 238, 239, 240, 267
Ferling, John 200, 202-204
Filegelman, Jay 137

Florida 84, 85, 154, 169, 170, 241, 271
Fort McHenry 211, 212, 223, 224, 268, 274
Foster, Augustus 226, 238
France 37, 60, 62, 64, 83, 84, 89, 142, 143, 150-176, 180-185, 192, 193, 201-202, 218, 258, 266
Franklin, Benjamin 73, 84, 89
Freeman, Morgan 137
French 62-65, 84, 151-152, 158-177, 186, 219, 259
French Directory 158, 160
French West Indies 152
Gage, Thomas 71
Gallatin, Albert 194-198, 228
George III 65, 66, 71, 72, 78
Georgetown 209
Georgia 62, 71, 112, 243
Germans 60
Gerry, Elbridge 159, 160, 166, 169
Ghent, Belgium 228, 229, 231, 232
Gilje, Paul 273
Goodrich, Samuel 215
Great Awakening 60-62
Great Lakes 65, 230, 240
Greek mythology 18
Greek-Persian War 20
Greeks 19, 20, 58
Greenland, 20
Gregorian Calendar 30-32
Gregory XIII 30, 31
Gregory, Saint 59
Grenville, George 67, 68
Griswold, Roger 163, 209
Halicarnassus 43

Halifax 230
Hamilton, Alexander 92, 144-147, 151-157, 161, 165, 169, 170, 174-178, 187, 200, 201, 208, 240
Hampstead Hill 224
Hancock, John 81, 89
Harper, Robert 173
Harrison, William Henry 186
Hartford Convention 234, 235, 245-250
Henry, Patrick 89, 90, 174
Herodotus 20, 21, 42-44, 51
Herodotus, *The Histories* 43-44
Hickey, David 229, 237, 265, 266
High Federalist 144, 145, 161, 167, 168, 169, 170, 174, 175, 177, 187, 200, 201
Historiography 22, 38, 45, 50, 51
Holland 83, 173
Holton, Woody 208
Holy Roman Empire 84
Howard, Hugh 273
Illinois 230
impressment 227, 228, 232, 238, 246
Independence Hall 88, 89
India 18
Indiana 230
indirect taxes 68, 69, 70
intolerable acts (see Coercive Acts) n70, 71
Ireland 82
Jackson, Andrew 233, 234, 241, 244, 245, 268, 271
Jackson, Helen Hunt 48
Jay, John 92, 152, 153

Jay's Treaty 153, 154, 157, 158
Jefferson, Thomas 55, 73, 78-79, 89, 97, 133, 141-142, 145-148, 151, 155-158, 160-161, 168, 172, 175, 177-185, 196, 199-204, 208-211, 217, 219, 238-239, 243, 245
John Bull 275
Kastor, Peter 274
Kentucky 167, 196, 234, 243, 245
Kentucky Resolution 167, 196-198
Key, Francis Scott 211, 212, 213, 214
King George's War 62
King, Rufus 239
Kurtz, Stephen 208
Labrador 240
Lake Champlain 220
Larson, Edward J. 200-202
Lee, Richard Henry 72, 89, 90
Leland, John 179
Lexington, Massachusetts 71, 74
Lincoln, Abraham 56, 125, 130, 131, 133, 148
Liverpool, Lord 231
Livingston, Robert 181, 182, 183
Livy 46
Locke, John 59, 136
Logan, George 166, 167
London, England 143, 226
loose constructionists 147
Lot 43
Louis XVI of France 151
Louisbourg, Fortress 62
Louisiana 142, 169, 180, 181, 183, 202, 209, 241, 243, 250
Louisiana Purchase 180, 209, 250
Loyalists 83, 85, 139, 269
Lyon, Matthew 162, 163, 209
Machiavelli, Niccole 47
Macon, Nathan 219
Madison, Dolly 221, 222
Madison, James 92, 148, 156, 168, 183-186, 202, 215, 221, 226-230, 235, 236, 239, 240, 243, 245, 273
Maier, Pauline 131, 136
Maine 229, 250
Marshall, John 158, 160
Massachusetts 62, 71, 87, 112, 166, 170, 179, 216, 242, 250
McCullough, David 173, 208
McHenry, James 168, 169, 174, 175
Meacham, Thomas 208
Means, Stephen, 40
mercantilism 86
Michigan 230
Milton, John 59
Minnesota 230
minutemen 71, 74
Mississippi 270, 271
Mississippi River 66, 84, 154, 181, 184, 230, 233, 252
Missouri 242, 243, 250, 251
Missouri Compromise 242, 243, 250-259

Monroe Doctrine 241, 242, 259-265, 272
Monroe, James 154, 181, 183, 202, 226, 239, 240-244, 259, 260 272
Morris, Robert 77, 81, 89
Mount Olympus 18
Mr. Madison's War 215, 239
Muller, Charles 273
Munger, George 274
Murray, William Vans 169, 171,172, 174
Myth 24-25, 41-42
Napoleon 180, 181, 203, 219, 220, 227, 229, 236, 268
Napoleonic Wars 203, 229
Natchez, Mississippi 270
National Intelligencer 217, 222
Native Americans (also Indians) 48, 63, 65, 66, 70, 111, 182, 186, 219, 230, 233, 237, 241, 248, 270, 271
Navigation Acts 67
Navy (US) 121, 221, 226, 273, 275
Navy (British) 152, 185, 217, 223, 224, 225, 226, 232, 260
New Hampshire 92, 112
New Jersey 112
New Orleans 181, 220, 233-235, 245, 268
New York 77, 79, 125, 152, 216, 218, 222, 235
Newfoundland 240
Nivola, Peter 274
North Carolina 72, 112, 224
Northwest Territory 154, 230
Norway 84
Nova Scotia 62

Ohio 63, 230
Ohio Valley 67, 245
Olive Branch Petition 72
oral history 49, 50
Orders in Council 226, 227
Oregon Territory 240
Otis, Harrison 173
Ottawa 65
Paine, Thomas 72, 93, 138
Paris, France 143, 159, 160
Parliament, British 67-71, 107, 109
Patapsco River 224
Patuxent River 220
Pekeham, Edward 233, 234
Pensacola, Florida 241
Pennsylvania 73, 77, 112, 125, 146, 166, 194, 201, 208
Philadelphia 71, 73-76, 81, 88-90, 92, 132, 143, 153, 154
Pickersgill, Caroline 212
Pickersgill, Mary Young 212
Pinckney, Charles Cotesworth 158, 159, 160, 183
Pinckney, Thomas 154, 155, 156,
Pinckney's Treaty 154
Pitt, William 64, 67
Plato 58
Plattsburgh Bay 225, 231
Polk, James K. 242
Pontiac 65
Pontiac's War 65-67
Portugal 84, 261, 264
Potomac River 222
primary sources 3, 15, 16, 21, 23, 25, 38, 44, 45, 51
Proclamation Line of 1763 65, 66, 138

Proclamation of Neutrality 151
project-based learning 22, 39, 50, 135, 206, 272
Protestant 59
Provisional Army 168
Prussia 62, 84
Quebec 230
Quincy, Massachusetts 166, 173
Ranke, Leopold von 47
Reconstruction, US 36
Republican Party 148, 177, 178, 217, 219, 239, 243
Republicans 148, 153-162, 165, 168, 170, 177, 179, 180, 192, 194, 199, 201, 202, 215-220, 239, 240, 266, 267, 269
Revere, Paul 71
Revolution of 1800 178, 199
Rhode Island 87, 88
Rip Van Winkle 104
Rodney, Caesar 75, 77
Roman Catholic Church 31
Ross, Robert 220, 223, 224
Rule of 1756 152, 153
Russell, Jonathan 226-228
Russia 83, 84, 227, 228, 260
Sarai (Sarah) 43
Saratoga 225
science 12, 18, 20, 21, 24, 25, 29, 48, 49
Scotland 82
Scots-Irish 60
Scottish Enlightenment 136
Second Bank of the United States 240
secondary sources 10, 38, 39, 46

Sedgwick, Theodore 170, 173
Sedition Act 162, 163, 165, 167, 177, 187-196
Selincour, Aubrey de 44
Seminoles 241
Senaca Falls, New York 79, 125
Seven Years' War 63, 66, 67, 74, 272
Shays, Daniel 87
Sherman, Roger 89
sine qua non 229
Smith, Gene Allen 266, 270-271
Sons of Liberty 68
South America 129, 169
South Carolina 73, 77, 112, 155, 156
Spain 31, 60, 62, 83, 84, 154, 180, 241, 261, 263-265
Spanish 62, 63, 154, 170, 241, 259, 271
St. Mark's, Florida 241
St. Petersburg 227, 228, 260
Stagg, J.C.A. 273
Stamp Act 68, 69
Stamp Act Congress 68
standing army 168, 236
Star Spangled Banner 213
status quo ante bellum 63, 232
Stricker, John 224
Stuart, Gilbert 210
Supreme Court 120, 152, 159
Talleyrand-Perigord, Charles Maurice de 159, 160, 169

Taylor, Alan 265, 266, 268-270
Tea Act 70
Tecumseh 186
The Hague 169
Thomson, Charles 89
To Anacreon in Heaven 213
Tonnant 211
Townshend, Charles 69
Transcontinental Treaty 241
Treaty of Aix-la-Chapelle 62-63
Treaty of Ghent 232-235, 239, 245, 267
Treaty of Paris (1763) 64
Treaty of Paris (1784) 84, 150
Trumbell, John 138
Ultra Federalists (also High Federalists) 143, 165, 203
Undeclared War (or Quasi-War) 176, 180, 218
uti possidetis 232
Vermont 162, 163,
Virginia 72, 73, 76, 89, 112, 142, 159, 167, 170, 174, 201, 234, 239, 243, 245,
Wallis, John 139
war hawks 166, 174, 177

War of Jenkin's Ear 62
War of Austrian Succession 62
War of Spanish Succession 63
Washington, Booker T. 8
Washington, DC 212, 220, 221, 222, 223, 225, 226, 234, 235
Washington, George 71, 92, 141, 143-153, 155, 157, 158, 161, 164, 165, 168, 170, 171, 175-177, 180, 183, 184, 185, 200-204, 208, 210
Whiskey Rebellion 146
Whiskey Tax 146, 148, 180
Whitefield, George 61
Wills, Gary 136
Wilson, James 89
Wilson, Norman J. 50, 51
Winder, William 221
Wisconsin 230
Woolf, Virginia 48
Writ of Habeas Corpus 122
XYZ Affair 159, 160, 162, 165, 168
Zaggarri, Rosemarie 200, 204-206

www.ingramcontent.com/pod-product-compliance
Lightning Source LLC
Chambersburg PA
CBHW060945230426
43665CB00015B/2068